JEWISH LEARNING INSTITUTE

ב״ה

TORAH STUDIES

Torah Studies

Season Three 5778

Student Textbook

The ROHR JEWISH LEARNING INSTITUTE
gratefully acknowledges
the pioneering support of

George & Pamela
Rohr

Since its inception,
the JLI has been
a beneficiary of the vision,
generosity, care, and concern
of the Rohr family.

In the merit of
the tens of thousands of hours
of Torah study
by JLI students worldwide,
may they be blessed with health,
Yiddishe nachas from all their loved ones,
and extraordinary success
in all their endeavors.

DEDICATED TO
Reb Zvi and Betty Ryzman

*With deep appreciation for their leadership
and partnership in teaching and bringing
Torah study to all corners of the world.*

*May they and their family enjoy health, happiness,
nachas, success, and abundance in all their
endeavors, as they go from strength to strength in
their service of G-d and the Jewish people.*

Contents

SHEMINI

Snake-Oil Salesman

Getting Off the Ground

PARSHAH OVERVIEW
Shemini

On the eighth day, following the seven days of their inauguration, Aaron and his sons begin to officiate as kohanim (priests); a fire issues forth from G-d to consume the offerings on the altar, and the divine presence comes to dwell in the Sanctuary.

Aaron's two elder sons, Nadav and Avihu, offer a "strange fire before G-d, which He commanded them not," and they die before G-d. Aaron is silent in the face of his tragedy. Moses and Aaron subsequently disagree as to a point of law regarding the offerings, but Moses concedes that Aaron is correct.

G-d commands the kosher laws, identifying the animal species permissible and forbidden for consumption. Land animals may be eaten only if they have split hooves and also chew their cud; fish must have fins and scales; a list of non-kosher birds is given, and so is a list of kosher insects (four types of locusts).

Also in Shemini are some of the laws of ritual purity, including the purifying power of the mikveh (a pool of water meeting specified qualifications) and the wellspring. Thus the people of Israel are enjoined to "differentiate between the impure and the pure."

The Snake Prohibition

The Laws of Kashrut

TEXT 1A

Vayikra (Leviticus) 11:27

> וְכֹל הוֹלֵךְ עַל כַּפָּיו בְּכָל הַחַיָּה הַהֹלֶכֶת עַל אַרְבַּע טְמֵאִים הֵם לָכֶם כָּל הַנֹּגֵעַ בְּנִבְלָתָם יִטְמָא עַד הָעָרֶב:

And among all the animals that walk on four legs, any [animal] that walks on its paws is unclean for you. Anyone who touches their carcasses will be unclean until evening.

TEXT 1B

Rashi, ad loc.

"עַל כַּפָּיו." כְּגוֹן כֶּלֶב וָדוֹב וְחָתוּל.

On its paws: such as a dog, a bear, or a cat.

Rabbi Shlomo Yitzchaki
(Rashi)
1040–1105
Most noted biblical and Talmudic commentator. Born in Troyes, France, Rashi studied in the famed *yeshivot* of Mainz and Worms. His commentaries on the Pentateuch and the Talmud, which focus on the straightforward meaning of the text, appear in virtually every edition of the Talmud and Bible.

TEXT 2A

Vayikra (Leviticus) 11:42

כֹּל הוֹלֵךְ עַל גָּחוֹן וְכֹל הוֹלֵךְ עַל אַרְבַּע עַד כָּל מַרְבֵּה רַגְלַיִם לְכָל הַשֶּׁרֶץ הַשֹּׁרֵץ עַל הָאָרֶץ לֹא תֹאכְלוּם כִּי שֶׁקֶץ הֵם:

Any [creature] that goes on its belly, and any [creature] that walks on four [legs] to any [creature] that has many legs, among all creeping creatures that creep on the ground, you shall not eat, for they are an abomination.

TEXT 2B

Talmud Tractate Chulin, 67b

Babylonian Talmud

A literary work of monumental proportions that draws upon the legal, spiritual, intellectual, ethical, and historical traditions of Judaism. The 37 tractates of the Babylonian Talmud contain the teachings of the Jewish sages from the period after the destruction of the Second Temple through the fifth century CE. It has served as the primary vehicle for the transmission of the Oral Law and the education of Jews over the centuries; it is the entry point for all subsequent legal, ethical, and theological Jewish scholarship.

תנו רבנן, 'הולך על גחון' – זה נחש; 'כל' – לרבות השילשול ואת הדומה לשילשול; 'על ארבע' – זה עקרב; 'כל הולך' – לרבות את החיפושית ואת הדומה לחיפושית; 'מרבה רגלים' – זה נדל; 'עד כל' – לרבות את הדומה ואת הדומה לדומה.

The rabbis taught in a baraita: "Any creature that goes on its belly" refers to a snake. The word "any" teaches us to include an earthworm in the prohibition. "Any creature that walks on four" refers to a scorpion. "Any creature that has many legs" refers to a centipede. The word "any" teaches us to include in the prohibition those that resemble them and those that resemble those that resemble them.

TEXT 2C

Rashi, Vayikra 11:42

"הולך על גחון." זה נחש ולשון גחון שחייה שהולך שח ונופל על מעיו.

"That goes on its belly." This is the snake. The word גחון denotes "bending low" [and it is used to describe the snake] because it moves while bent in a prostrated posture, prostrated on its belly.

The Primeval Snake

TEXT 3

Bereishit (Genesis) 3:14

וַיֹּאמֶר ה' אֱלֹקִים אֶל הַנָּחָשׁ כִּי עָשִׂיתָ זֹּאת אָרוּר אַתָּה מִכָּל הַבְּהֵמָה
וּמִכֹּל חַיַּת הַשָּׂדֶה עַל גְּחֹנְךָ תֵלֵךְ וְעָפָר תֹּאכַל כָּל יְמֵי חַיֶּיךָ:
וְאֵיבָה אָשִׁית בֵּינְךָ וּבֵין הָאִשָּׁה וּבֵין זַרְעֲךָ וּבֵין זַרְעָהּ הוּא יְשׁוּפְךָ רֹאשׁ
וְאַתָּה תְּשׁוּפֶנּוּ עָקֵב:

And the Lord G-d said to the serpent, "Because you have done this, cursed be you more than all the cattle and more than all the beasts of the field; you shall walk on your belly, and you shall eat dust all the days of your life.

"And I shall place hatred between you and between the woman, and between your seed and between her seed. He will crush your head, and you will bite his heel."

TEXT 4

Talmud Tractate Sotah, 9a-b

תנו רבנן . . שכל הנותן עיניו במה שאינו שלו מה שמבקש אין
נותנין לו ומה שבידו נוטלין הימנו.

וכן מצינו בנחש הקדמוני שנתן עיניו במה שאינו ראוי לו מה
שביקש לא נתנו לו ומה שבידו נטלוהו ממנו.

אמר הקדוש ברוך הוא אני אמרתי יהא מלך על כל בהמה וחיה
ועכשיו ארור הוא מכל הבהמה ומכל חית השדה אני אמרתי יהלך
בקומה זקופה עכשיו על גחונו ילך אני אמרתי יהא מאכלו מאכל
אדם עכשיו עפר יאכל הוא אמר אהרוג את אדם ואשא את חוה
עכשיו איבה אשית בינך ובין האשה ובין זרעך ובין זרעה.

The sages taught in a baraita ... Anyone who places his eyes on that which is not his is not given what he desires, and that which he had is taken from him.

And, so we find with the primeval snake who placed his eyes on that which was unfit for him [because he wanted to marry Eve]. Consequently, that which he desired was not given to him, and that which was in his possession was taken from him.

The Holy One, Blessed be He, said: I initially said that the snake would be king over every animal and beast, but now he is cursed more than all the animals and beasts of the field.

I initially said that the snake would walk upright, but now he shall go on his belly; I said that his food would

*be the same as the food eaten by a person, but now
he shall eat dust. The snake said: I will kill Adam and
marry Eve, but now, "I will put enmity between you
and the woman and between your seed and her seed."*

How the Evil Inclination Works

The Satan and the Snake

TEXT 5

Zohar, vol. I, 35b

Zohar

The seminal work of kabbalah, Jewish mysticism. The *Zohar* is a mystical commentary on the Torah, written in Aramaic and Hebrew. According to the Arizal, the *Zohar* contains the teachings of Rabbi Shimon bar Yocha'i, who lived in the Land of Israel during the second century. The *Zohar* has become one of the indispensable texts of traditional Judaism, alongside and nearly equal in stature to the Mishnah and Talmud.

כתיב "והנחש היה ערום", דא יצר הרע.

The verse states, "Now the serpent was cunning." This refers to the evil inclination.

The Great Lie

TEXT 6

Rabb Shalom Dovber Schneersohn of Lubavitch,
Kuntres Umaayon, Discourse 1, ch. 1-2

Rabbi Shalom Dovber Schneersohn
(Rashab)
1860–1920
Chasidic rebbe. Rabbi Shalom Dovber became the fifth leader of the Chabad movement upon the passing of his father, Rabbi Shmuel of Lubavitch. He established the Lubavitch network of *yeshivot* called Tomchei Temimim. He authored many volumes of Chasidic discourses and is renowned for his lucid and thorough explanations of kabbalistic concepts.

הִנֵּה בְּסֵפֶר הַשָּׁרָשִׁים בְּשֹׁרֶשׁ שָׂטָה פֵּירֵשׁ שְׂטִים מִלְּשׁוֹן הַטָּיָה . . . וְעַל שֵׁם זֶה נִקְרָא הַיֵּצֶר הָרָע שָׂטָן עַל שֵׁם שֶׁמַּשְׁטֶה וּמַטֶּה אֶת הָאָדָם מִדֶּרֶךְ הַטּוֹב . . . וְזֶהוּ גַם כֵּן מַה שֶׁמְּפָרֵשׁ בַּמִּדְרָשׁ שְׂטִים לְשׁוֹן שְׁטוּת כִּי עִנְיַן הַשְּׁטוּת הוּא הַהַטָּיָה מִדֶּרֶךְ הָאֱמֶת וְכֵן מָצִינוּ בְּדִבְרֵי רַבּוֹתֵינוּ זִכְרוֹנָם לִבְרָכָה שֶׁחִבְּרוּ ב' עִנְיָנִים אֵלּוּ, וְכִדְאִיתָא בַּגְּמָרָא (סוֹטָה ג. א) עַל פָּסוּק כִּי תִשְׂטֶה אִשְׁתּוֹ אֵין אָדָם עוֹבֵר עֲבֵירָה אֶלָּא אִם כֵּן נִכְנַס בּוֹ רוּחַ שְׁטוּת, הֲרֵי שֶׁהַשְּׁטָה וּשְׁטוּת הוּא עִנְיָן אֶחָד, שֶׁהוּא הַהַטָּיָה מִדֶּרֶךְ הָאֱמֶת וְדֶרֶךְ הַטּוֹב . . .

וְהָעִנְיָן הוּא דְּהִנֵּה מַה שֶׁהָאָדָם בָּא לַעֲבוֹר עַל דַּרְכֵי הַתּוֹרָה וּלְהַמְשֵׁךְ אַחֲרֵי תַּאֲווֹת לִבּוֹ לְהִתְעַנֵּג בְּתַעֲנוּגֵי בְּנֵי אָדָם . . . הוּא עַל יְדֵי הֲסָתַת הַיֵּצֶר הָרָע לוֹמַר לוֹ כִּי טוֹב לְפָנָיו דָּבָר זֶה וְכִי תַאֲוָה הוּא לָעֵינַיִם, וּכְמוֹ שֶׁכָּתוּב בְּחֵטְא עֵץ הַדַּעַת "וַתֵּרֶא הָאִשָּׁה כִּי טוֹב הָעֵץ לְמַאֲכָל וְכִי תַאֲוָה הוּא לָעֵינַיִם כו' וַתִּקַּח מִפִּרְיוֹ וַתֹּאכַל וַתִּתֵּן גַּם לְאִישָׁהּ עִמָּהּ וַיֹּאכַל".

וּבֶאֱמֶת הוּא שְׁטוּת נוֹרָא וְכִי זֶהוּ הַטּוֹב אֲשֶׁר אֵלָיו יִמְשׁוֹךְ הָאָדָם בְּחִיר הַנִּבְרָאִים.

Sefer Hasharashim *defines the root-word* shitah *as "divergence"… Accordingly, the evil inclination is called* Satan, *for it causes one to "veer" from the right path … This is why the Midrash associates the word* shitim *with the word* shtut *[folly], for folly is the departure from the way of truth.*

Indeed, our sages of blessed memory joined these two ideas, as the Talmud states,… "A person does not sin unless a spirit of folly enters him," meaning that "divergence" is the same idea as folly, which is the departure from the way of truth and the way of good. … This means that when a person wishes to transgress the ways of Torah, and to follow after the desire of his heart in all the humanly pleasures . . . it is the result of his evil inclination telling him that this pleasure before him is something good, and that "it is a delight to the eyes." As it is written with regard to the sin of the Tree of Knowledge, "And the woman saw that the tree was good for food and that it was a delight to the eyes . . . so she took of its fruit, and she ate, and she gave also to her husband with her, and he ate."

In truth, such a perception is a terrible folly, for is this the goodness a human being—the chosen of all creatures—ought to pursue?

The Conditioning Process

TEXT 7

Talmud Tractate Shabbat, 105b

שֶׁכָּךְ אוּמָּנְתוֹ שֶׁל יֵצֶר הָרַע הַיּוֹם אוֹמֵר לוֹ עֲשֵׂה כָּךְ וּלְמָחָר אוֹמֵר לוֹ
עֲשֵׂה כָּךְ עַד שֶׁאוֹמֵר לוֹ עֲבוֹד עֲבוֹדָה זָרָה וְהוֹלֵךְ וְעוֹבֵד.

That is the craft of the evil inclination. Today it tells him do this, and tomorrow it tells him do that, until eventually, it tells him to worship idols and he goes and worships idols.

Physical Indulgence, Spiritual Desensitization

TEXT 8

Rabbi Shalom Dovber Schneersohn of Lubavitch,
Kuntres Umaayon, Discourse 2, ch. 1

וְיָדוּעַ דְּהַתּוֹקֶף דְּנֶפֶשׁ הַבַּהֲמִית גּוֹרֵם חֲלִישׁוּת הַנֶּפֶשׁ הָאֱלֹקִית,
וּכְמַאֲמָר תּוּקְפָּא דְּגוּפָא חוּלְשָׁא דְּנִשְׁמָתָא, דְּתוֹקֶף הַחוּמְרִיּוּת
דְּהַנֶּפֶשׁ הַבַּהֲמִית גּוֹרֵם חֲלִישׁוּת הַנֶּפֶשׁ הָאֱלֹקִית.
דְּלָא מִיבָּעְיָא שֶׁמִּתְרַחֵק מְאֹד מִתּוֹרָה וַעֲבוֹדָה שֶׁבְּלֵב זוֹ תְּפִלָּה, דְּאֵינוֹ
שַׁיָּיךְ כְּלָל שֶׁיִּבִין אֵיזֶה עִנְיָן אֱלֹקִי, וְיִתְבּוֹנֵן בּוֹ וְיוּרְגַּשׁ הָעִנְיָן הָאֱלֹקִי

בְּנַפְשׁוֹ עַד שֶׁיִּתְפָּעֵל בִּבְחִינַת הַמְשָׁכַת הַלֵּב לְדָבְקָה בּוֹ וּלְהִכָּלֵל בֶּאֱלֹקוּת כו' דְּלְכָל זֶה אֵינוֹ שַׁיָּךְ כְּלָל וּכְלָל.

דְּלָא מִיבָּעְיָא שֶׁמִּתְרַחֵק מְאֹד מִתּוֹרָה וַעֲבוֹדָה שֶׁבַּלֵּב זוֹ תְּפִלָּה, דְּאֵינוֹ שַׁיָּךְ כְּלָל שֶׁיָּבִין אֵיזֶה עִנְיָן אֱלֹקִי, וְיִתְבּוֹנֵן בּוֹ וְיִרְגַּשׁ הָעִנְיָן הָאֱלֹקִי בְּנַפְשׁוֹ עַד שֶׁיִּתְפָּעֵל בִּבְחִינַת הַמְשָׁכַת הַלֵּב לְדָבְקָה בּוֹ וּלְהִכָּלֵל בֶּאֱלֹקוּת כו' דְּלְכָל זֶה אֵינוֹ שַׁיָּךְ כְּלָל וּכְלָל.

אֶלָּא שֶׁגַּם זֹאת שֶׁאֵין פַּחַד אֱלֹקִים נֶגֶד עֵינָיו וְשׁוֹכֵחַ עַל אֱלֹקוּת עַד שֶׁמַּה שֶׁהַדָּבָר הַהוּא הוּא נֶגֶד רְצוֹן הוי', אֵינוֹ מוֹנֵעַ וּמְעַכֵּב אוֹתוֹ מֵעֲשִׂיָּתוֹ, מִפְּנֵי שֶׁאֵין הָאֱלֹקוּת וּרְצוֹנוֹ יִתְבָּרֵךְ נִרְגָּשׁ בְּנַפְשׁוֹ לְהִתְפָּעֵל מִזֶּה.

וְעִם הֱיוֹת שֶׁאֵינוֹ כּוֹפֵר חַס וְשָׁלוֹם בַּה' וְתוֹרָתוֹ וְיוֹדֵעַ שֶׁהַתּוֹרָה אֱמֶת וְשֶׁזֶּה אָסוּר עַל פִּי הַתּוֹרָה, אָמְנָם גַּם כֵּן אֵינוֹ נִרְגָּשׁ בְּנַפְשׁוֹ הָאִיסּוּר, שֶׁזֶּה יִהְיֶה לוֹ מְנִיעָה וְעִכּוּב וְשֶׁיּוּכַל לַעֲמוֹד נֶגֶד רוּחַ תַּאֲוָתוֹ כו'.

וְכָל זֶה הוּא מִפְּנֵי רִיבּוּי הַשִּׁיקּוּעַ בְּתַאֲווֹת הַיְתֵּר הֲרֵי הַנֶּפֶשׁ הַבַּהֲמִית שֶׁלּוֹ נִתְגַּבֵּר בְּיוֹתֵר, וְהַנֶּפֶשׁ הָאֱלֹקִית נֶחֱלָשׁ בְּיוֹתֵר, וְלָזֹאת כְּשֶׁהַנֶּפֶשׁ הַבַּהֲמִית מְסִיתוֹ וּמַרְאֶה לוֹ טוּב הַדָּבָר, הִנֵּה עִם הֱיוֹתוֹ דְּבַר אִיסּוּר מַמָּשׁ הֲרֵי הוּא נִמְשָׁךְ אַחֲרָיו וְנִכְשָׁל בָּזֶה רַחֲמָנָא לִצְלָן.

וּבָזֶה מוּבָן בִּפְשִׁיטוּת אֵיךְ הוּא זֶה שֶׁמַּמְשִׁיטָה אֶת עַצְמוֹ בְּטוּב הַדָּבָר שֶׁהֲרֵי הוּא רַע גָּמוּר וּמוֹרִיד אֶת נַפְשׁוֹ מְאֹד עַל יְדֵי זֶה רַחֲמָנָא לִצְלָן.

It is well known that an over-nurtured animal soul weakens the G-dly soul, as the saying goes, "Strong body, weak soul," namely, intense corporeality of the animal soul weakens the G-dly soul.

When this occurs, one drifts away from Torah prayer—for it is impossible for such a person to truly understand and meditate upon G-dly concepts, and be *driven by them to cleave to G-d, etc. All this is completely out of such a person's league.*

But aside from that, this spiritual numbness causes one to lose fear of G-d, to forget about G-dliness so that the fact that something opposes G-d's will doesn't stop him from doing it, for G-d and His will are not tangibly felt in the soul.

Though one doesn't deny the existence of G-d and the truth of the Torah, G-d forbid, and he knows the Torah is true and that the matter at hand is forbidden by the Torah, he doesn't feel the prohibition in a way that prevents him from doing it or that motivates him to overcome his desires, etc.

This is because over-engrossment in permissible pleasures has greatly bolstered his animal soul, and consequently greatly weakened his G-dly soul. Therefore, when his animal soul tempts him and shows him the allure of the forbidden matter, though it is outright forbidden, he is drawn after it and succumbs, G-d forbid.

It is thus understood quite simply how one is tricked into the false goodness of something that in truth is utterly evil, which drags the soul far down, G-d forbid.

Keep Your Head Up High

Purpose of Man

TEXT 9

Rabbi Shalom Dovber Schneersohn of Lubavitch,
Kuntres Umaayon Discourse 1, ch. 3

דְּהִנֵּה כָּל דָּבָר שֶׁנִּבְרָא בָּעוֹלָם הוּא לְצוֹרֶךְ אֵיזֶה תַּכְלִית, וְתַכְלִית כָּל
דָּבָר הוּא כְּשֶׁעוֹלֶה לְמַעְלָה מִמַּדְרֵיגַת עַצְמוֹ.
וּכְמוֹ תַּכְלִית הַצּוֹמֵחַ הוּא כְּשֶׁנִּכְלָל בְּחַי, וְתַכְלִית הַחַי הוּא כְּשֶׁנִּכְלָל
בִּמְדַבֵּר וְתַכְלִית הַמְדַבֵּר הוּא כַּאֲשֶׁר רוּחוֹ עוֹלֶה לְמַעְלָה וְנִכְלָל
בְּמַדְרֵיגוֹת הָרוּחָנִיּוֹת שֶׁלְּמַעְלָה מִמֶּנּוּ.

Everything that was created in this world serves some purpose, and that purpose is to ascend to a level higher than its own. For example, the purpose of a plant is fulfilled when it is consumed and thus elevated by animal, and the purpose of the animal is fulfilled when it is consumed and elevated by man, and the purpose of man is fulfilled when his spirit is elevated to and one with the spiritual levels that are above him.

Varying Types of Pleasure

TEXT 10

Ibid., ch. 2-3

כִּי הִנֵּה יֵשׁ כַּמָּה מִינֵי תַעֲנוּגִים, וּכְמוֹ הַתַּעֲנוּג בְּמַאֲכָל עָרֵב וּמָתוֹק
לַחֵיךְ שֶׁזֶּהוּ תַעֲנוּג הַיּוֹתֵר שָׁפָל וּפָחוּת . . . שֶׁזֶּהוּ תַעֲנוּג בַּהֲמִי מַמָּשׁ,
שֶׁהַבְּהֵמָה נִמְשֶׁכֶת אַחֲרֵי דְבָרִים הַטּוֹבִים וְהָעֲרֵבִים לְפִי טִבְעָהּ וְאֵינָהּ
יוֹדַעַת מָטוֹב אַחֵר כִּי אִם מֵהַטּוֹב הַזֶּה וְאַחֲרָיו הִיא נִמְשֶׁכֶת.
וּלְמַעֲלָה מִזֶּה הוּא כְּמוֹ הַתַּעֲנוּג בְּקוֹל עָרֵב שֶׁהוּא תַעֲנוּג רוּחָנִי יוֹתֵר.
וּלְמַעֲלָה מִזֶּה הוּא הַתַּעֲנוּג בְּעִנְיָנֵי הַמִּדּוֹת, וּכְמוֹ בְּמִדַּת הַטּוֹב וְהַחֶסֶד
שֶׁעוֹשֶׂה עִם זוּלָתוֹ שֶׁיֵּשׁ בָּזֶה תַּעֲנוּג נִפְלָא לְהָאִישׁ הַטּוֹב.

. . . וְהִנֵּה לְמַעְלָה מִכָּל הַתַּעֲנוּגִים הַנַּ"ל הוּא הַתַּעֲנוּג שֶׁבַּשֵׂכֶל וְהַחָכְמָה
וּכְמוֹ בְּהַמְצָאַת אֵיזֶה הַשְׂכָּלָה חֲדָשָׁה שֶׁיֵּשׁ בָּזֶה תַּעֲנוּג נִפְלָא, וְכֵן
בְּהַשָּׂגָה וַהֲבָנָה כְּשֶׁלּוֹמֵד אֵיזֶה עִנְיָן וּמֵבִינוֹ בְּטוֹב, שֶׁיֵּשׁ בָּזֶה תַּעֲנוּג
הַנֶּפֶשׁ, וְזֶהוּ הַטּוֹב וְהַתַּעֲנוּג אֲמִיתִי וְהַנַּעֲלֶה בֶּאֱמֶת)וּבִתְנַאי שֶׁהַחָכְמָה
עַצְמָהּ טוֹבָה וַאֲמִיתִּית הִיא, כִּי אִם הַחָכְמָה הִיא רַע מִצַּד עַצְמָהּ הֲרֵי
הִיא מִכְּלַל הַדְּבָרִים הָאֲסוּרִים שֶׁאָסוּר לַעֲסוֹק בָּהּ.)

וְהָאָדָם בַּאֲשֶׁר הוּא בְּחִיר הַנִּבְרָאִים צָרִיךְ לִהְיוֹת הַטּוֹב וְהַתַּעֲנוּג שֶׁלּוֹ
בְּעִנְיָנִים הָרוּחָנִים דַּוְקָא, וּבִפְרָט בְּעִנְיָנֵי הַחָכְמָה, וּבָזֶה דַּוְקָא יִהְיֶה
עֹנֶג נַפְשׁוֹ כִּי זוֹהִי מַעֲלָתוֹ עַל כָּל הַנִּבְרָאִים בְּהַשֵּׂכֶל שֶׁנִּיתַּן לוֹ וְנַפְשׁוֹ
הִיא נֶפֶשׁ הַמַּשְׂכֶּלֶת.

וּבִפְרָט מִצַּד הַנֶּפֶשׁ הָאֱלֹקִית שֶׁבּוֹ שֶׁהִיא מִבְּחִינַת הַחָכְמָה הָעֶלְיוֹנָה
כַּיָּדוּעַ, וְצָרִיךְ לִהְיוֹת כָּל הַמְשָׁכַת נַפְשׁוֹ וְכָל חֶפְצוֹ וּמְגַמָּתוֹ בְּעֵסֶק
חָכְמַת הַתּוֹרָה וּבָזֶה תִּתְעַנֵּג נַפְשׁוֹ וְעַל יְדֵי זֶה תִּתְעַלֶּה נַפְשׁוֹ בְּעִילּוּי
הַמַּעֲלָה וְהַמַּדְרֵגָה אֲשֶׁר לְכַךְ הוּא נִבְרָא.

There are various types of pleasures, such as the pleasure of eating tasty food, which is the lowliest pleasure . . . it is truly animalistic, for an animal pursues only what it naturally perceives as good and enjoyable; it doesn't know of any goodness other than this.

Above this is a more spiritual pleasure, such as listening to beautiful music.

Above this is the pleasure that comes with fine character traits, such as the tremendous pleasure from doing acts of goodness and kindness for another person.

Now, above all these pleasures is the pleasure found in intellect and wisdom, such as in developing a new idea, which brings tremendous pleasure. Likewise, grasping and properly understanding a concept brings great pleasure to the soul, and this is the true and ultimate goodness and pleasure (on condition that the wisdom itself is good and true, for if it is evil wisdom, it is forbidden to study it.)

The goodness and pleasure of man, as the chosen of all creatures, must be in such spiritual matters, and specifically in matters of wisdom; this ought to be one's soul's pleasure, for this is what places man above all other creatures—the intellect he has.

And specifically from the perspective of the G-dly soul, which stems from G-d's wisdom, one ought to pursue the wisdom of Torah and find its pleasure therein.

One's soul will thereby be elevated to the exalted level for which it was created.

Studying G-dly Concepts

TEXT 11

Rabbi Shalom Dovber Schneersohn of Lubavitch,
Torat Shalom, pp. 256-258

The very fact of understanding the concepts of Cha-sidut in the mind—even before working to apply the concepts to one's divine service—transforms one's faculties from corporeal to G-dly. By understanding G-dliness through abstract application of the soul's fac-ulties, these faculties become G-dly….When one finds himself on a faraway island, remote from any other people, and does nothing but contemplate concepts of Chasidut, *he is greatly elevated. Through his involve-ment in* Chasidut *he becomes removed from corporeal-ity and becomes G-dly. When he contemplates such subjects, he truly is higher and loses his connection to the physical.*

Avoiding the Belly

TEXT 12

Rashi, Vayikra 11:42

"הולך על גחון." זה נחש ולשון גחון שחייה שהולך שח ונופל
על מעיו.

"That goes on its belly." This is the snake. The word גחון denotes "bending low" [and it is used to describe the snake] because it moves while bent in a prostrated posture, prostrated on its belly.

TEXT 13

The Lubavitcher Rebbe, Likutei Sichot, vol. 17, p. 122

Rabbi Menachem Mendel Schneerson
1902–1994

The towering Jewish leader of the 20th century, known as "the Lubavitcher Rebbe," or simply as "the Rebbe." Born in southern Ukraine, the Rebbe escaped Nazi-occupied Europe, arriving in the U.S. in June 1941. The Rebbe inspired and guided the revival of traditional Judaism after the European devastation, impacting virtually every Jewish community the world over. The Rebbe often emphasized that the performance of just one additional good deed could usher in the era of Mashiach. The Rebbe's scholarly talks and writings have been printed in more than 200 volumes.

נאר אין דעם איז דא א הוראה אין עבודת ה'; חז"ל זאגן אויף נחש "דא יצה"ר". און דאס זאגט תורה: דער יצה"ר קומט ניט לכתחילה באווירקן א אידן ער זאל ווערן א "הולך על מעיו"—גיין, קריכן און ליגן אין עניני אכילה וכו' ענינים ארציים. ער הייבט אן מיט "הולך שח": זיין קאפ איז אראפגעלאזט, איינגעבויגן, עם פעלט אים אין שאו מרום עיניכם ראו וגו'—אבער דאס דערפירט, אז סוכ"ס ווערט ער ר"ל א "נופל על מעיו". ווי חז"ל זאגן "כך אומנתו של יצה"ר היום אומר לו עשה כך וכו' (ביז) עבוד ע"ז".

און דערפאר איז די עצה ווי צו בייקומען דעם "נחש" איז דורך ליגן אין ענינים פון מרום—תורה בכלל, ובמיוחד אין נסתר ופנימיות התורה.

The sages teach that the snake "is the evil inclination." The Torah is telling us that the evil inclination's first step is not to turn a person into one who "walks on his belly," but rather to turn a person into one who "moves while bent in a prostrated posture." This means [that] a person whose head hangs lowly, lacks the [the ability to] "Raise up your eyes and see [Who created all this]."

But ultimately, this results, G-d forbid, in one who "falls on his belly." As the sages have said, "That is the craft of the evil inclination. Today it tells him do this, [and tomorrow it tells him do that, until eventually, it tells him] to worship idols."

The solution to withstand[ing] the [the influence of the] "snake" is by staying involved with lofty matters—the study of Torah, and specifically the study of the innermost parts of Torah.

2

<small>T</small>AZRIA <small>M</small>ETZORA

Check Your Privilege

Getting Ahead in Life

PARSHAH OVERVIEW
Tazria Metzora

The parashiyot *of Tazria and Metzora continue the discussion of the laws of* tumah v'taharah, *ritual impurity and purity.*

A woman giving birth should undergo a process of purification, which includes immersing in a mikveh *(a naturally gathered pool of water) and bringing offerings to the Holy Temple. All male infants are to be circumcised on the eighth day of life.*

Tzaraat *(often mistranslated as "leprosy") is a supranatural plague, which can afflict people as well as garments or homes. If white or pink patches appear on a person's skin (dark pink or dark green in garments or homes), a* kohen *is summoned. Judging by various signs, such as an increase in size of the afflicted area after a seven-day quarantine, the* kohen *pronounces it* tamei *(impure) or* tahor *(pure).*

A person afflicted with tzaraat *must dwell alone outside of the camp (or city) until he is healed. The afflicted area in a garment or home must be removed; if the* tzaraat *recurs, the entire garment or home must be destroyed.*

When the metzora *("leper") heals, he or she is purified by the* kohen *with a special procedure involving two birds, spring water in an earthen vessel, a piece of cedar wood, a scarlet thread, and a bundle of hyssop.*

Ritual impurity is also engendered through a seminal or other discharge in a man, and menstruation or other discharge of blood in a woman, necessitating purification through immersion in a mikveh.

Who's on First?

Animals First

TEXT 1A

Vayikra (Leviticus) 11:4

אַל תְּשַׁקְּצוּ אֶת נַפְשֹׁתֵיכֶם בְּכָל הַשֶּׁרֶץ הַשֹּׁרֵץ וְלֹא תִטַּמְּאוּ בָּהֶם
וְנִטְמֵתֶם בָּם:

You shall not make yourselves abominable with any creeping creature that creeps, and you shall not defile yourselves with them, that you should become impure through them.

TEXT 1B

Ibid., 11: 4

לְהַבְדִּיל בֵּין הַטָּמֵא וּבֵין הַטָּהֹר וּבֵין הַחַיָּה הַנֶּאֱכֶלֶת וּבֵין הַחַיָּה אֲשֶׁר
לֹא תֵאָכֵל:

To distinguish between the impure and the pure, and between the animal that may be eaten and the animal that may not be eaten.

TEXT 2

Rashi, Vayikra 11:4

אמר רב שמלאי: כשם שיצירתו של אדם אחר כל בהמה חיה ועוף
במעשה בראשית, כך תורתו נתפרשה אחר תורת בהמה חיה ועוף.

Rabbi Simlai said, "Just as the human was created after all domestic animals, wild beasts, and birds, so too, the laws of human purity are stated after the laws about the purity of domestic animals, wild beasts, and birds."

Rabbi Shlomo Yitzchaki (Rashi)
1040–1105
Most noted biblical and Talmudic commentator. Born in Troyes, France, Rashi studied in the famed *yeshivot* of Mainz and Worms. His commentaries on the Pentateuch and the Talmud, which focus on the straightforward meaning of the text, appear in virtually every edition of the Talmud and Bible.

TEXT 3

Talmud Tractate Sanhedrin, 38a

תנו רבנן: אדם נברא בערב שבת, ומפני מה?...
שאם תזוח דעתו עליו אומר לו: יתוש קדמך במעשה בראשית...
דבר אחר: כדי שיכנס לסעודה מיד. משל למלך בשר ודם שבנה
פלטרין ושיכללן, והתקין סעודה, ואחר כך הכניס אורחין.

Our rabbis taught: Adam was created last of all beings on Friday afternoon, on the eve of Shabbat.

And why? . . .

If he becomes too proud, he may be reminded that the gnats preceded him in the order of creation.

Babylonian Talmud
A literary work of monumental proportions that draws upon the legal, spiritual, intellectual, ethical, and historical traditions of Judaism. The 37 tractates of the Babylonian Talmud contain the teachings of the Jewish sages from the period after the destruction of the Second Temple through the fifth century CE. It has served as the primary vehicle for the transmission of the Oral Law and the education of Jews over the centuries; it is the entry point for all subsequent legal, ethical, and theological Jewish scholarship.

Another answer: That he might go directly to the banquet. The matter may be compared to a human king who built a palace, furnished it, and prepared a banquet, and only then did he usher in the guests.

TEXT 4

Rashi, Bereishit 1:1

"בראשית ברא אלקים." אין המקרא הזה אומר אלא דרשני, כמו שדרשוהו רבותינו ז"ל בשביל התורה שנקראת "ראשית דרכו," ובשביל ישראל שנקראו "ראשית תבואתו".

The first words in the Torah, "In the beginning," call for an allegorical interpretation.

Our rabbis taught that G-d created the world for two purposes that are characterized as beginnings. For the Torah, which is called "the beginning of His way," and for the Jewish people, who are called "the first of His grain."

TEXT 5

The Lubavitcher Rebbe, Likutei Sichot, vol. 7, pp. 75-77

Rabbi Menachem Mendel Schneerson
1902–1994

The towering Jewish leader of the 20th century, known as "the Lubavitcher Rebbe," or simply as "the Rebbe." Born in southern Ukraine, the Rebbe escaped Nazi-occupied Europe, arriving in the U.S. in June 1941. The Rebbe inspired and guided the revival of traditional Judaism after the European devastation, impacting virtually every Jewish community the world over. The Rebbe often emphasized that the performance of just one additional good deed could usher in the era of Mashiach. The Rebbe's scholarly talks and writings have been printed in more than 200 volumes.

דער סדר אין תורה, דאס הייסט ווי א איד הייבט אן לערנען תורה, איז מן הקל אל הכבד. סיי אין תוכן הלימוד, "בן חמש למקרא, בן עשר למשנה כו'", און אין זיי גופא, "ילמוד אדם תורה ואחר כך יהגה". סיי אין אופן הלימוד: מען הייבט ניט אן גלייך פון למוד התורה לשמה אין דעם העכסטען אופן . . . נאר כפסק חכמינו זכרונם לברכה, "מעיקרא, כי עביד איניש, אדעתא דנפשיה קא עביד" . . .

און פונקט ווי דער סדר ביי כללות הלימוד פון תורה איז מלמטה למעלה, אזוי איז אויך דער סדר פון לימוד הפרשיות: פריער קומען די גרינגערע ענינים און ערשט שפעטער די שווערערע. און דערפאר איז תורתו נתפרשה אחר תורת בהמה חיה ועוף, וויל דער בירור, דער "להבדיל בין הטמא ובין הטהור" פון בהמה חיה ועוף, וויבאלד אז אינם יכולים לעבור כלל על רצונו יתברך, איז זייער בירור גרינגער ווי דער בירור פון אדם.

The order of Torah study is from minor to major. This pertains to the subject of study; "At the age of five, one studies the written Torah, at the age of ten, one graduates to the more complex oral Torah." Within this order, one studies the basic concepts first, and then graduates to in-depth analyses. It also pertains to the purpose of Torah study. As our sages declared, "In the beginning, one studies for one's own sake," and then graduates to altruistic study for the sake of G-d . . .

G-d gave the Torah in similar order: First the lighter subjects and then the more challenging subjects. The laws of animal purity precede the laws of human purity because it is easier to "separate the impure from the pure animal" than to maintain the purity of the human. This is because the animal is incapable of defying G-d's will, whereas the human is eminently capable.

Body and Soul

TEXT 6

The Lubavitcher Rebbe, Sefer Hamaamarim, 5710, p. 15

ירידת הנשמה בגוף אינה בשביל עצמה, דהנשמה עצמה אינה
צריכה תיקון. וכל ענין ירידתה הוא בשביל לתקן ולזכך ולברר את
הגוף ונפש הטבעית . . .
דהנשמה קודם שירדה להתלבש בגוף ונפש הטבעית הרי היתה
בתכלית הדביקות במקור חוצבה, באלוקים חיים, והיתה בדביקות
אמיתי ודביקות תמידי בלי שום פירוד כלל. והיינו שהיתה ברצון
אחד להוי' בלבדו, ואין זר אתו.

The soul's descent into the body is not for its own sake inasmuch as the soul does not require repair. Its sole purpose in descending to the body is to repair, cleanse, and make the body and its physical vitality transparent to G-d.

Before the soul descended to the body, it was in absolute attachment to its source, the living G-d. It was in a state of true and constant attachment without any separation at all. Its sole desire was for G-d and none other.

TEXT 7A

Talmud Tractate Pesachim, 62b

> רבי שמלאי אתא לקמיה דרבי יוחנן, אמר ליה: ניתני לי מר
> ספר יוחסין.
> אמר ליה: מהיכן את?
> אמר ליה: מלוד.
> והיכן מותבך?
> בנהרדעא.
> אמר ליה: אין נידונין לא ללודים ולא לנהרדעים, וכל שכן דאת
> מלוד ומותבך בנהרדעא!

Rabbi Simlai approached Rabbi Yochanan and asked to be taught the Book of Genealogy.

Rabbi Yochanan: Where are you from?

Rabbi Simlai: From Lod.

Rabbi Yochanan: And where do you currently reside?

Rabbi Simlai: In Naharda'a.

Rabbi Yochanan: We do not teach Lodites nor Na-hardeans. We certainly cannot teach you for you are both a Lodite by birth and a Nahardean by residence.

TEXT 7B

Rashi, ad loc.

לדחוייה איכוון.
לישנא אחרינא: לפי שאינן מיוחסין

He intended to put him off.

Another explanation: Lodites and Nahardeans lack pedigree.

TEXT 8

Likutei Sichot, vol. 7, pp. 76-77

א מעלה פון א זאך קען קומען אין צויי אופנים: א) אז מ' גיט עס
מלמעלה—צי מצד התולדה, אדער מען גיט עס במתנה לאחרי
היצירה: מען האט אבער אויף דעם ניט געהארעוועט. ב) מצד
עבודה: מען הארעוועט אויף דעם און מען פארדינט עס.
אין יעדען פון די צויי אופנים איז פאראן א יתרון מיוחד: אין די
מעלות פון ערשטען סוג איז דא א יתרון, וואס די מעלות זיינען ניט

קיין באגרעניצטע: וויבאלד זיי קומען מלמעלה, האבען זיי ניט אויף
זיך קיינע הגבלות: אנדערש ווי עס זיינען די מעלות וועלכע קומען
דורך עבודה.

לאידך גיסא, האבען אין זיך די מעלות וואס קומען דורך עבודת
האדם א יתרון דערמיט וואס זיי זיינען **בפנימיותו:** די עניינים וועלכט
מען באקומט במתנה מלמעלה אדער מען האט זיי מצד התולדה,
וויבאלד דער מקבל האט אויף זיי ניט געהארעוועט, קען זיין אז ער
איז צו זיי קיין כלי ניט, ובמילא רירען זיי עם ניט אן אין זיין פנימיות.
מה שאין כן, די מעלות וועלכע **ער** האט אויסגעהארעוועט, רירען
זיי אן, און זיי זיינען פארבונדען, און זיי גייען אריין בפנימיותו.

*The value of a personal strength can come in two ways:
(a) it can be given from above—either as a birthright
or as a post-birth gift. Either way, this strength is not
achieved through personal toil, or (b) it can be earned
through toil and labor.*

*Each of these possibilities carries a benefit: The first
kind of strength is advantageous because it is not
commensurate with the limitations of our toil. Since
these gifts come from above, they are without limit,
as opposed to strengths that we achieve through hard
work, which are commensurate with our toil.*

*Conversely, strengths for which we toil have the
advantage of affecting us deeply. Strengths that we
receive as gifts from above or by birthright might fail
to touch us deeply since we did not work for them.
However, strengths for which we toil, touch us deeply
and become part of us.*

TEXT 9

The Lubavitcher Rebbe, Sefer Hasichot 5725, vol. 2, p. 7

רבי יוחנן האט מורא געהאט אז וויבאלד רב שמלאי איז ניט קיין
מיוחס, איז ביי אים דא א נטיה למעט במעלת היוחסין, וועט ער
דעריבער לערנען דעם חלק אין תורה וואו עס רעדט זיך וועגען
יוחסין, ניט ווי עס דארף צו זיין. דעריבער האט ער מיט עם ניט
געוואלט לערנען יוחסין, ווייל דאס איז אן ענין פון "לפני עוור לא
תתן מכשול".

Rabbi Yochanan was concerned that Rabbi Simlai, who did not come from a prominent family, might be inclined to minimize the benefits of pedigree. If so, he might inadvertently study the Torah's Book of Genealogy with something less than proper regard. Rabbi Yochanan hesitated to teach this subject to Rabbi Simlai because the Torah prohibits placing "a stumbling block before the blind."

Check Your Privilege

TEXT 10

"Learning Something from Everything," Dovid Shraga Polter, Chabad.org

The Rebbe once told a story of Rabbi Shneur Zalman of Liadi, known as the Alter Rebbe, and his grandchild, Menachem Mendel, who later gained renown as the Tzemach Tzedek.

The Alter Rebbe once offered the boy a once-in-a-lifetime opportunity of blessing him with the knowledge of the entire Torah. At any given time, he could refer to any part of the Torah and it would be right at his fingertips. Amazingly, the boy refused to accept the gift. Having been blessed with deep insight beyond his years, he felt that he did not want his knowledge of Torah to be received effortlessly — for the mitzvah is to toil *in Torah.*

Years later, the Tzemach Tzedek deeply regretted his previous decision. "With [the knowledge of] all the teachings of Torah with which my grandfather offered to bless me, there would always be more to uncover and probe! Why then did I not accept the unique gift from my grandfather? It would have allowed me to expand my inner abilities and strengths to take yet a greater leap into the infinite sea of Torah."

3

ACHAREI-KEDOSHIM

The Curious Case of the Scapegoat

Absolving Guilt, Restoring Dignity

PARSHAH OVERVIEW
Acharei-Kedoshim

Following the deaths of Nadav and Avihu, G-d warns against unauthorized entry "into the holy." Only one person, the Kohen Gadol ("High Priest"), may—but once a year, on Yom Kippur—enter the innermost chamber in the Sanctuary to offer the sacred ketoret to G-d.

Another feature of the Day of Atonement service is the casting of lots over two goats, to determine which should be offered to G-d and which should be dispatched to carry off the sins of Israel to the wilderness.

The Parshah of Acharei also warns against bringing korbanot (animal or meal offerings) anywhere but in the Holy Temple, forbids the consumption of blood, and details the laws prohibiting incest and other deviant sexual relations.

The Parshah of Kedoshim begins with the statement: "You shall be holy, for I, the L-rd your G-d, am holy." This is followed by dozens of mitzvot (divine commandments) through which the Jew sanctifies him- or herself and relates to the holiness of G-d.

These include: the prohibition against idolatry, the mitzvah of charity, the principle of equality before the law, Shabbat, sexual morality, honesty in business, honor and awe of one's parents, and the sacredness of life.

Also in Kedoshim is the dictum that the great sage Rabbi Akiva called a cardinal principle of Torah, and of which Hillel said, "This is the entire Torah, the rest is commentary"—"Love your fellow as yourself."

A Tale of Two Goats

The Yom Kippur Lottery

TEXT 1A

Vayikra (Leviticus) 16:7-10

וְלָקַח אֶת שְׁנֵי הַשְּׂעִירִם וְהֶעֱמִיד אֹתָם לִפְנֵי ה' פֶּתַח אֹהֶל מוֹעֵד:
וְנָתַן אַהֲרֹן עַל שְׁנֵי הַשְּׂעִירִם גּוֹרָלוֹת גּוֹרָל אֶחָד לַה' וְגוֹרָל אֶחָד לַעֲזָאזֵל:
וְהִקְרִיב אַהֲרֹן אֶת הַשָּׂעִיר אֲשֶׁר עָלָה עָלָיו הַגּוֹרָל לַה' וְעָשָׂהוּ חַטָּאת:
וְהַשָּׂעִיר אֲשֶׁר עָלָה עָלָיו הַגּוֹרָל לַעֲזָאזֵל יָעֳמַד חַי לִפְנֵי ה' לְכַפֵּר עָלָיו
לְשַׁלַּח אֹתוֹ לַעֲזָאזֵל הַמִּדְבָּרָה:

And he shall take the two he-goats and place them before the Lord at the entrance to the Tent of Meeting.

And Aaron shall place lots upon the two he-goats: one lot "for G-d," and the other lot, "for Azazel."

And Aaron shall bring the he-goat upon which the lot "for G-d" came up, and designate it as a sin offering.

And the he-goat upon which the lot "for Azazel" came up shall be placed while still alive, before G-d, to [initiate] atonement upon it and to send it away to Azazel, into the desert.

TEXT 1B

Ibid., 16:21-22

וְסָמַךְ אַהֲרֹן אֶת שְׁתֵּי [יָדָיו] עַל רֹאשׁ הַשָּׂעִיר הַחַי וְהִתְוַדָּה עָלָיו אֶת
כָּל עֲוֹנֹת בְּנֵי יִשְׂרָאֵל וְאֶת כָּל פִּשְׁעֵיהֶם לְכָל חַטֹּאתָם וְנָתַן אֹתָם עַל
רֹאשׁ הַשָּׂעִיר וְשִׁלַּח בְּיַד אִישׁ עִתִּי הַמִּדְבָּרָה:
וְנָשָׂא הַשָּׂעִיר עָלָיו אֶת כָּל עֲוֹנֹתָם אֶל אֶרֶץ גְּזֵרָה וְשִׁלַּח אֶת
הַשָּׂעִיר בַּמִּדְבָּר:

And Aaron shall lean both of his hands [forcefully] upon the live he-goat's head and confess upon it all the willful transgressions of the Children of Israel, all their rebellions, and all their unintentional sins, and he shall place them on the he-goat's head and send it off to the desert with a timely man.

The he-goat shall thus carry upon itself all their sins to a precipitous land, and he shall send off the he-goat into the desert.

The Process

TEXT 2A

Maimonides, Mishneh Torah, Hilchot Avodat Yom Hakippurim, 3:1-4

Rabbi Moshe ben Maimon
(Maimonides, Rambam)
1135–1204
Halachist, philosopher, author, and physician. Maimonides was born in Córdoba, Spain. After the conquest of Córdoba by the Almohads, he fled Spain and eventually settled in Cairo, Egypt. There, he became the leader of the Jewish community and served as court physician to the vizier of Egypt. He is most noted for authoring the *Mishneh Torah*, an encyclopedic arrangement of Jewish law, and for his philosophical work, *Guide for the Perplexed*. His rulings on Jewish law are integral to the formation of halachic consensus.

שני הגורלות אחד כתוב עליו להשם ואחד כתוב עליו לעזאזל . . . טרף בקלפי והעלה שני הגורלות בשתי ידיו לשם שני השעירים ופותח ידיו . . . ונותן שני הגורלות על שניהם, של ימין על ימין ושל שמאל על של שמאל . . .

וקושר לשון זהורית משקל שתי סלעים בראש שעיר המשתלח ומעמידו כנגד בית שלוחו.

There were two lots: upon one was written "for G-d" and upon the other "for Azazel ... He would quickly grab the lots from the kalpi *(urn for drawing lots) and lift up the two lots in his two hands for the two goats. He would open his hands ...He would then place the two lots on the two goats, the lot in his right hand on the goat to his right and the lot in his left on the goat to his left ...*

He ties a crimson cord weighing two selaim *on the head of the goat to be sent to Azazel and positions it in the direction where it will be sent.*

TEXT 2B

Ibid., 3:7

ואחר כך משלח את השעיר החי ביד איש המוכן להוליכו למדבר
. . . וסוכות היו עושין מירושלים עד תחלת המדבר, ושובת איש
אחד או אנשים הרבה בכל סוכה וסוכה מהן כדי שיהיו מלוין אותו
מסוכה לסוכה, על כל סוכה וסוכה אומרין לו הרי מזון והרי מים, אם
כשל כחו וצריך לאכול אוכל, ומעולם לא הוצרך אדם לכך, ואנשי
הסוכה האחרונה עומדין בסוף התחום ורואין את מעשיו מרחוק.
כיצד היה עושה חולק לשון של זהורית שבקרניו, חציו קושר בסלע
וחציו קושר בין שתי קרניו, ודוחפו לאחוריו והוא מתגלגל ויורד, לא
היה מגיע לחצי ההר עד שהוא נעשה איברים איברים, ובא ויושב
לו תחת סוכה האחרונה עד שתחשך, ודרכיות היו עושין ומניפין
בסודרין כדי שידעו שהגיע שעיר למדבר.

Afterward, he would send the living goat to be taken to the desert with a person prepared for this task. . . . Booths were built on the way from Jerusalem to the desert. One person or many people would spend the day in each booth so that they would accompany him from booth to booth. In each booth, they would say, "Here is food and here is water." If he became weak and it was necessary for him to eat, he would eat, but no one ever required this. The people in the last booth would stand at the end of the Sabbath limits and watch his actions from a distance.

What would he do? He would divide the crimson cord tied to the goat's horns. He would tie half to a rock and half between its two horns. He would then push it backward, and it would roll over and descend. It would not reach half of the mountain before it was broken into separate limbs. He would then sit in the last booth until nightfall. Sentries would be positioned along the way who would wave flags so that the people in the Temple would know that the goat reached the desert.

The Crimson Wool

TEXT 3A

Mishnah Tractate Yoma, 6:8

Mishnah
The first authoritative work of Jewish law that was codified in writing. The Mishnah contains the oral traditions that were passed down from teacher to student; it supplements, clarifies, and systematizes the commandments of the Torah. Due to the continual persecution of the Jewish people, it became increasingly difficult to guarantee that these traditions would not be forgotten. Rabbi Yehudah Hanasi therefore redacted the Mishnah at the end of the second century. It serves as the foundation for the Talmud.

רַבִּי יִשְׁמָעֵאל אוֹמֵר . . . לָשׁוֹן שֶׁל זְהוֹרִית הָיָה קָשׁוּר עַל פִּתְחוֹ שֶׁל הֵיכָל, וּכְשֶׁהִגִּיעַ שָׂעִיר לַמִּדְבָּר הָיָה הַלָּשׁוֹן מַלְבִּין, שֶׁנֶּאֱמַר, "אִם יִהְיוּ חֲטָאֵיכֶם כַּשָּׁנִים כַּשֶּׁלֶג יַלְבִּינוּ".

Rabbi Yishmael stated … A strip of crimson wool was tied to the door of the Hechal, *and when the goat reached the wilderness, the crimson wool turned white, as it is written, "Though your sins be as scarlet, they shall be as white as snow."*

TEXT 3B

Talmud Tractate Yoma, 67a

תנו רבנן בראשונה היו קושרין לשון של זהורית על פתח האולם
מבחוץ הלבין היו שמחין לא הלבין היו עצבין ומתביישין התקינו
שיהיו קושרין על פתח אולם מבפנים ועדיין היו מציצין ורואין
הלבין היו שמחין לא הלבין היו עצבין התקינו שיהיו קושרין אותו
חציו בסלע וחציו בין קרניו.

Babylonian Talmud
A literary work of monumental proportions that draws upon the legal, spiritual, intellectual, ethical, and historical traditions of Judaism. The 37 tractates of the Babylonian Talmud contain the teachings of the Jewish sages from the period after the destruction of the Second Temple through the fifth century CE. It has served as the primary vehicle for the transmission of the Oral Law and the education of Jews over the centuries; it is the entry point for all subsequent legal, ethical, and theological Jewish scholarship.

Our sages taught: At first they would tie this strip of crimson to the opening of the Entrance Hall of the Temple on the outside. If the strip turned white, they would rejoice [as this indicated that their sins had been atoned for]. If it did not turn white, they would be sad and ashamed.

[When the sages saw that people were overly distressed on Yom Kippur,] they established that they should tie the strip of crimson to the opening of the entrance hall on the inside [because only a few could actually go in to see it]. And they would still peek and see: If it turned white, they would rejoice, and if it did not turn white, they would be sad. Therefore, the sSages established that they should tie half of the strip to the rock and half of it between the goat's horns [so that the people would not know what happened to the strip until after the conclusion of Yom Kippur].

Fodder for the Scoffers

TEXT 4

Talmud Tractate Yoma, 67b

את חוקותי תשמרו דברים שהשטן משיב עליהן ואלו הן אכילת
חזיר ולבישת שעטנז וחליצת יבמה וטהרת מצורע ושעיר המשתלח
ושמא תאמר מעשה תוהו הם תלמוד לומר אני ה' אני ה' חקקתיו
ואין לך רשות להרהר בהן.

"And my statutes you shall keep"—these are things that the Satan laughs at: abstaining from eating pork, from wearing shatnez, *the* chalitzah *ceremony, purification of a leper, and the dispatching of the Azazel goat. Lest you say they are nonsense, it is therefore written, "I am the Lord your G-d." I have commanded it; you have no right to question.*

What Does This All Mean

TEXT 5

Rashi, Vayikra 16:8

"עֲזָאזֵל." הוּא הַר עַז וְקָשֶׁה, צוּק גָּבוֹהַ, שֶׁנֶּאֱמַר (פָּסוּק כב) אֶרֶץ גְּזֵרָה, חֲתוּכָה.

"*Azazel.*" *This refers to [a] rough and hard mountain; a high cliff. As the verse states, "[The he-goat shall thus carry upon itself all their sins to] a precipitous land.*"

Rabbi Shlomo Yitzchaki
(Rashi)
1040–1105
Most noted biblical and Talmudic commentator. Born in Troyes, France, Rashi studied in the famed *yeshivot* of Mainz and Worms. His commentaries on the Pentateuch and the Talmud, which focus on the straightforward meaning of the text, appear in virtually every edition of the Talmud and Bible.

Exception to the Rules of Sacrifices

TEXT 6

Maimonides, Mishneh Torah, Hilchot Maaseh Hakorbanot 18:1-2

כל הקרבנות כולן בין קרבנות בהמה ועוף בין קרבנות מנחות מצות
עשה להקריבן בבית הבחירה שנאמר ושם תעשה כל אשר אנכי
מצוך וכן מצות עשה להיות כל אדם מטפל ומביא קרבנות בהמה
שנתחייב להקריבן מחוצה לארץ לבית הבחירה שנאמר קדשיך
אשר יהיו לך ונדריך תשא וגו' מפי השמועה למדו שאינו מדבר אלא
בקדשי חוצה לארץ שהוא מטפל בהם עד שיביאם לבית הבחירה:
המקריב קרבן חוץ לעזרה ביטל מצות עשה ועבר על לא תעשה
שנאמר השמר לך פן תעלה עולותיך בכ"מ אשר תראה ואם הקריב
במזיד חייב כרת שנאמר אשר יעלה עולה או זבח ואל פתח אהל
מועד לא הביאו ונכרת מעמיו בשוגג מביא חטאת קבועה:

*There is a positive commandment to offer all of the
sacrifices—whether sacrifices of animals or fowl or
meal-offerings—in G-d's chosen house, as the verse
states, "There you will perform everything that I
command you." Similarly, it is a positive commandment for a person to make the effort to bring animal
sacrifices that he is obligated to bring and transport
them from the Diaspora to G-d's chosen house, as the
verse states, "[Only] your sacraments that you possess
and your vows shall you bear . . . [to the place that
G-d will choose]." According to the Oral Tradition, we
have learned that [the verse] is speaking only about*

sacrificial animals from the Diaspora that he takes the effort to deal with until he brings them to G-d's chosen house.

One who offers a sacrifice outside the Temple Court-yard negates a positive commandment and violates a negative commandment, as the verse states, "Take heed lest you offer your burnt-offerings in any place that you see." If he offered a sacrifice [in such a place] willfully, he is liable for karet, as the verse states, "[Any man] . . . who will offer a burnt-offering or a sacrifice, but did not bring it to the Tent of Meeting . . . he will be cut off from his people." If he transgressed unknowingly, he must bring a fixed sin-offering.

Keeping the Satan Quiet

A Simple Solution

TEXT 7

Maimonides, The Guide for the Perplexed 3: 46

> ואין ספק לאדם שהחטאים אינם משאות שיעתקו מגב איש אחד
> לגב איש אחר, אבל אלו המעשים כולם משלים להביא מורא בנפש
> עד שתתפעל לתשובה, כלומר שכל מה שקדם ממעשינו נקינו
> ממהם והשלכנום אחרי גוינו והרחקנום תכלית ההרחקה.

There is no doubt that sins cannot be carried like a burden—and taken off the shoulder of one being to be laid on that of another being. Rather, these ceremonies are of a symbolic character and serve to impress men with a certain idea and to induce them to repent; as if to say, "we have freed ourselves of our previous deeds, have cast them behind our backs, and removed them from us as far as possible."

The Hint

TEXT 8A

Rabbi Avraham ibn Ezra, ibn Ezra Vayikra 16:8

אם יכולת להבין הסוד שהוא אחר מלת עזאזל תדע סודו וסוד
שמו, כי יש לו חברים במקרא. ואני אגלה לך קצת הסוד ברמז
בהיותך בן שלשים ושלש תדענו.

If you can understand the secret behind the word Azazel, you will understand its hidden meaning and the hidden meaning of its name. Indeed, there are similar words in the Torah. I will partially reveal the secret by way of a hint: When you are thirty-three years old, you will understand it.

Rabbi Avraham ibn Ezra
1092–1167

Biblical commentator, linguist, and poet. Ibn Ezra was born in Toledo, Spain, and fled the Almohad regime to other parts of Europe. It is believed that he was living in London at the time of his death. Ibn Ezra is best known for his literalistic commentary on the Pentateuch. He also wrote works of poetry, philosophy, medicine, astronomy, and other topics.

The Demons

TEXT 8B

Vayikra (Leviticus) 17:7

וְלֹא יִזְבְּחוּ עוֹד אֶת זִבְחֵיהֶם לַשְּׂעִירִם אֲשֶׁר הֵם זֹנִים אַחֲרֵיהֶם חֻקַּת
עוֹלָם תִּהְיֶה זֹּאת לָהֶם לְדֹרֹתָם:

And they shall no longer slaughter their sacrifices to the se'irim *after which they stray. This shall be an eternal statute for them, for [all] their generations.*

The Link

TEXT 9A

Nachmanides, Pirush Haramban to Vayikra 16:8

Rabbi Moshe ben Nachman
(Nachmanides, Ramban)
1194–1270
Scholar, philosopher, author, and physician. Nachmanides was born in Spain and served as the leader of Iberian Jewry. In 1263, he was summoned by King James of Aragon to a public disputation with Pablo Cristiani, a Jewish apostate. Though Nachmanides was the clear victor of the debate, he had to flee Spain because of the resulting persecution. He moved to Israel and helped reestablish communal life in Jerusalem. He authored a classic commentary on the Pentateuch and a commentary on the Talmud.

אמרו בבראשית רבה "ונשא השעיר עליו", זה עשו שנאמר "הן עשו אחי איש שעיר", את כל עונותם, עונות תם שנאמר "ויעקב איש תם".

Bereishit Rabah *explains the verse "The he-goat [se'ir] shall thus carry upon itself all their sins [avonotam]." This means that Esav—who is called se'ir—will bear the sins of the people of Jacob, who is called tam [i.e., avonot-tam].*

The Pacifier

TEXT 9B

Ibid.

ומפורש מזה בפרקי רבי אליעזר הגדול, לפיכך היו נותנין לו לסמאל שוחד ביום הכפורים שלא לבטל את קרבנם, שנאמר גורל אחד לה' וגורל אחד לעזאזל, גורלו של הקדוש ברוך הוא לקרבן עולה, וגורלו של עזאזל שעיר החטאת וכל עונותיהם של ישראל עליו, שנאמר ונשא השעיר עליו. ראה סמאל שלא נמצא בהם חטא ביום הכפורים, אמר לפני הקדוש ברוך הוא, רבון כל העולמים יש לך עם אחד בארץ כמלאכי השרת שבשמים, מה מלאכי השרת יחפי רגל כך הן ישראל יחפי רגל ביום הכפורים. מה מלאכי השרת אין בהם אכילה ושתיה כך ישראל אין בהם אכילה ושתיה ביום הכפורים. מה מלאכי השרת אין להם קפיצה כך ישראל עומדין על רגליהם ביום הכפורים. מה מלאכי השרת שלום מתווך ביניהם כך הן ישראל שלום מתווך ביניהם ביום הכפורים. מה מלאכי השרת נקיים מכל חטא כך הן ישראל נקיים מכל חטא ביום הכפורים. והקדוש ברוך הוא שומע עדותן של ישראל מן הקטיגור שלהם ומכפר על המזבח ועל המקדש ועל הכהנים ועל כל עם הקהל שנאמר וכפר את מקדש הקדש וגו', ע"כ אגדה זו. והנה הודיענו שמו ומעשהו:

It is explained in Pirkei Rabbi Eliezer Hagadol *that a "bribe" is given to Samael on Yom Kippur so that he doesn't try to nullify their offering to G-d, as the verse states, "One lot 'for G-d" and the other lot "for Azazel."… Azazel's portion is the sin-offering-goat,* which bears upon it all the sins of Israel, as the verse states, "The he-goat shall thus carry upon itself [all their sins]."

Samael would thus see on Yom Kippur that there is no sin among Israel, and would say to G-d, "Master of the Universe, You have one nation on the earth that is like the angels of heaven: Just as the angels are barefoot, Israel is barefoot on Yom Kippur. Just as the angels don't eat or drink, the people of Israel don't eat or drink on Yom Kippur. . . . Just as the angels are free of all sin, the people of Israel are free of all sin on Yom Kippur."

G-d would hear this praise of the Jewish people coming from their prosecuting angel and would atone for the altar, for the Temple, for the kohanim, and for the entire congregation.

Not a Sacrifice

TEXT 9C

Ibid.

והנה התורה אסרה לגמרי קבלת אלהותם וכל עבודה להם, אבל צוה הקדוש ברוך הוא ביום הכפורים שנשלח שעיר במדבר לשר המושל במקומות החרבן, והוא הראוי לו מפני שהוא בעליו ומאצילות כחו יבא חורב ושממון כי הוא העילה לכוכבי החרב והדמים והמלחמות והמריבות והפצעים והמכות והפירוד והחרבן ... וחלקו מן האומות הוא עשו שהוא עם היורש החרב והמלחמות, ומן הבהמות השעירים והעזים, ובחלקו עוד השדים הנקראים ... בלשון הכתוב "שעירים", כי כן יקרא הוא ואומתו שעיר. ואין הכונה בשעיר המשתלח שיהיה קרבן מאתנו אליו חלילה, אבל שתהיה כונתנו לעשות רצון בוראנו שצונו כך:

The Torah utterly forbids all forms of idol worship, but G-d commanded *the Jewish people to send on Yom Kippur a goat to the desert, to the minister who governs places of desolation, and the goat is best suited to Samael because he is its owner, as he is the source of destruction and desolation. He causes the fate of the sword, of blood, war, and strife, of injury and affliction, divisiveness and destruction...he takes his place among the nations in Esav [Se'ir], inheritor of the sword and battle.*

Among animal life, he takes its place among the goats—se'irim. Likewise, he is associated with the demons...called se'irim *in the Torah, for he and his nation are called Se'ir.*

Now, the purpose of the scapegoat is not to serve as a sacrifice from us to this spirit, G-d forbid. Rather, the purpose is to fulfill the will of G-d Who has commanded us so.

TEXT 9D

Ibid.

והמשל בזה, כמי שעשה סעודה לאדון וצוה האדון את האיש
העושה הסעודה תן מנה אחת לעבדי פלוני, שאין העושה הסעודה
נותן כלום לעבד ההוא ולא לכבודו יעשה עמו, רק הכל נתן לאדון
והאדון נותן פרס לעבדו, ושמר זה מצותו ועשה לכבוד האדון כל
אשר צוהו, ואמנם האדון לחמלתו על בעל הסעודה רצה שיהיו כל
עבדיו נהנין ממנה שיספר בשבחו ולא בגנותו:

*This can be understood by way of the following anal-
ogy: There was once a ruler who hosted a banquet.
During the banquet, he ordered his chamberlain to
give a certain one of his servants a portion of food.
Now, in doing so, the chamberlain did not actually
give anything of his own to that servant, nor did he
accord any honor to that servant. Rather, everything
the chamberlain did was for his master, and it is the
master who provided that servant with food by way
of the chamberlain who merely fulfilled his command.*

*Why did the master have the chamberlain give that
servant food? So that all the servants would be satis-
fied with the chamberlain's work and praise him rather
than criticize him.*

Guilt vs. Shame

Take Your Sins Back

TEXT 10

Rabbi Moshe Alshich, Vayikra 16:21

Rabbi Moshe Alshich
1508–1593

Biblical exegete. Rabbi Alshich was born in Turkey and moved to Safed, Israel, where he became a student of Rabbi Yosef Caro, the preeminent codifier of Jewish law. Alshich's biblical, homiletical, and ethical teachings remain popular to this day, most notably, *Torat Moshe*, a commentary on the Torah. His students included Rabbi Chaim Vital and Rabbi Yom Tov Tsahalon. He is buried in Safed.

וזה מאמר הכתוב וסמך אהרן את שתי ידיו וכו' והתודה עליו את כל עונות בני ישראל ואת כל פשעיהם לכל חטאתם. ונתן אותם על ראש השעיר, שהוא כי על ידי הסמיכה הוא נותן ממש אותם על ראש השעיר, כי כל המשחיתים שנעשו בהם ניתנים על ראשו. ועל כן לא יאות ינתנו על מזבח ה'. רק ושלח ביד איש עתי המדברה אל שורשה. והוא, כי כל עון ופשע וחטאה אשר יחטא איש הוא תת כח בטומאת השטן המחטיאו. ועל ידי החטא ההוא יפרד האיש מהקדושה וימשך טומאה מבחינת העון ההוא מטומאת מחטיאו אל נפשו. ועל כן בבא יום הכפורים עם התשובה, הלא מה שתשובה תולה ויום הכפורים מכפר מספיק להשמיט הכחות טומאת אשמותיו מנפשו, כמשים יד החלק להעביר המוץ כנזכר במאמר שבהקדמה השנית.

When the high priest leans his hands on the Azazel goat to confess the sins of the Jewish people, he, in fact, places those sins upon the goat, namely all the negative forces created by those sins are placed upon the goat.

Therefore, it would be inappropriate for this goat to be offered on the altar of G-d. Rather, it is sent to the desert to its source. For when a person sins, power is given to the impure forces of the Satan, which enticed him to commit that sin. The sin thus separates the sinner from holiness and draws upon him impurity from that sin.

Coupled with his repentance, the power of the Yom Kippur day achieves the removal of those negative forces.

Sin Is Part of the Plan

TEXT 11

Talmud Tractate Berachot, 32a

אמר רבי חמא ברבי חנינא אלמלא שלש מקראות הללו נתמוטטו רגליהם של שונאי ישראל חד דכתיב ואשר הרעותי וחד דכתיב "הנה כחומר ביד היוצר כן אתם בידי בית ישראל" וחד דכתיב "והסירותי את לב האבן מבשרכם ונתתי לכם לב בשר".

Rabbi Chama, son of Rabbi Chanina, said: Had it not been for these three verses, the legs of the enemies of Israel [a euphemism for Israel itself] would have collapsed, [as Israel would have been unable to withstand G-d's judgment].

One is the verse just mentioned in which it is written, "Those whom I have dealt in wickedness." And one is the verse in which it is written: "Behold, like clay in the potter's hand, so are you in My hand, House of Israel." And one is the verse in which it is written, "And

I will give you a new heart and a new spirit I will place within you, and I will remove the heart of stone from your flesh, and I will give you a heart of flesh."

TEXT 12

Rabbi Tzadok Hakohen Rabinowitz of Lublin, Tzidkat HaTzadik §40

Rabbi Tsadok Hakohen Rabinowitz of Lublin
1823–1900

Chasidic master and thinker. Rabbi Tsadok was born into a Lithuanian rabbinic family and later joined the Chasidic movement. He was a follower of the Chasidic leaders Rabbi Mordechai Yosef Leiner of Izbica and Rabbi Leibel Eiger. He succeeded Rabbi Eiger after his passing and became a rebbe in Lublin, Poland. He authored many works on Jewish law, Chasidism, kabbalah, and ethics, as well as scholarly essays on astronomy, geometry, and algebra.

עיקר התשובה הוא עד שיאיר ה' עיניו שיהיו זדונות כזכיות, רצה לומר שיכיר ויבין שכל מה שחטא היה גם כן ברצון השם יתברך, כמו שאמרו ז"ל שלושה פסוקים וכו' ואתה הסבות את לבם אשר הרעותי וגו', וכטעם ידיעה ובחירה שביאר האריז"ל בסוף ספר ארבע מאות שקל כסף, ששניהם אמת כל אחד במקום בפני עצמו במקום הבחירה שם אין מקום לידיעה, ובמקום הידיעה שם באמת אין מקום לבחירה, וכשמשיג לאור זה העצום אז שבו כל זדונותיו בלתי יוצאים מעומק ידיעת השם יתברך והוא ודעתו ורצונו הכל אחד:

ומאחר שהשם יתברך רצה כן הרי הכל זכיות וזוכה לכפרה גמורה שביום הכפורים שזה סוד השעיר לעזאזל שאילו עשוהו האדם עצמו היה עובד עבודה זרה גמור והוא לא יהיה, שהוא יסוד כל המצוות לא תעשה, וכל העבירות וההסרות מרצון השם יתברך. רק שהשעיר הוא על ידי רצון השם יתברך שהוא מצווה לשלחו לו נעשה עוד מצוה ולא עבירה. וכך פירשוהו חז"ל (פרקי דרבי אליעזר פרק מ"ו) ועיין ברמב"ן פרשת אחרי שאנו נותנים חלק לעזאזל שהוא הרע מצד מה שהשם יתברך צוה לתת לו ונמצא העבירה מצוה.

Real teshuvah *is when one is enlightened by G-d to the point that his sins are transformed into merits, meaning that one comes to recognize and understand that even one's sins come about by design, as the rabbis taught in the Talmud regarding the three verses…This is related to the teaching of the Arizal that the space of G-dly cognizance is indeed mutually exclusive to the space of free will. Where there is divine cognizance, there is indeed no free will. When one reached this lofty space, all of his previous sins are returned to G-d's cognizance. And, after all, G-d, His cognition, and His desire are all one.*

Inasmuch as one's sin is also part of the divine plan, this realization transforms the sins into merits, so that one achieves full atonement on Yom Kippur. This is the esoteric meaning of the Azazel goat. Were the goat to be selected and sent by man, it would amount to idol worship, a sin that is the basis for all the prohibitions of the Torah and for everything that transgresses G-d's will.

But the ceremony was, in fact, performed by G-d's will. He commanded to send the goat, which therefore amounts to a mitzvah rather than a sin. This is how the matter was explained by the sages of blessed memory. Also, see Nachmanides's explanation of the matter, namely that we send a portion to the evil of Azazel because G-d has thus commanded. It emerges that what would otherwise be a sin is, in fact, a mitzvah.

Two Aspects of Yom Kippur

TEXT 13

Vayikra (Leviticus) 16:30

כִּי בַיּוֹם הַזֶּה יְכַפֵּר עֲלֵיכֶם לְטַהֵר אֶתְכֶם מִכֹּל חַטֹּאתֵיכֶם לִפְנֵי יְהוָה תִּטְהָרוּ. כִּי בַיּוֹם הַזֶּה יְכַפֵּר עֲלֵיכֶם לְטַהֵר אֶתְכֶם מִכֹּל חַטֹּאתֵיכֶם לִפְנֵי יְהוָה תִּטְהָרוּ.

On this day you shall have all your sins atoned [yechaper], so that you will be cleansed [le-taher]. Before G-d you will be cleansed of all your sins.

TEXT 14

Talmud Tractate Berachot, 10a

הנהו בריוני, דהוו בשבבותיה דרבי מאיר והוו קא מצערו ליה טובא; הוה קא בעי רבי מאיר רחמי עלייהו כי היכי דלימותו; אמרה ליה ברוריא דביתהו: מai דעתך, משום דכתיב יתמו חטאים—מי כתיב 'חוֹטאים'? 'חטאים' כתיב! ועוד: שפיל לסיפיה דקרא: ורשעים עוד אינם: כיון דיתמו חטאים—ורשעים עוד אינם! אלא בעי רחמי עלייהו דלהדרו בתשובה—ורשעים עוד אינם! בעא רחמי עלייהו והדרו בתשובה.

There were hooligans in Rabbi Meir's neighborhood who caused him a great deal of anguish. Rabbi Meir prayed for G-d to have mercy on them, that they should die. Rabbi Meir's wife, Beruriah, said to him: What is your thinking? On what basis do you pray for the death of these hooligans? Do you base yourself on the verse, as it is written: "Let sins cease from the land"? But is it written, let sinners cease? Let sins cease, is written.

Moreover, go to the end of the verse, where it says: "And the wicked will be no more." If, as you suggest, "transgressions shall cease" refers to the demise of the evildoers, how is it possible that the wicked will be no more, i.e., that they will no longer be evil? Rather, pray for G-d to have mercy on them, that they should repent, as if they repent, then the wicked will be no more, as they will have repented.

[Rabbi Meir saw that Beruriah was correct, and] he prayed for G-d to have mercy on them, and they repented.

4

EMOR

"I'll Take Care of It"

Investing in Our Relationship with the Divine

PARSHAH OVERVIEW
Emor

The Torah section of Emor ("Speak") begins with the special laws pertaining to the kohanim ("priests"), the Kohen Gadol ("High Priest"), and the Temple service: A kohen may not become ritually impure through contact with a dead body, save on the occasion of the death of a close relative. A kohen may not marry a divorcee, or a woman with a promiscuous past; a Kohen Gadol can marry only a virgin. A kohen with a physical deformity cannot serve in the Holy Temple, nor can a deformed animal be brought as an offering.

A newborn calf, lamb, or kid must be left with its mother for seven days before being eligible for an offering; one may not slaughter an animal and its offspring on the same day.

The second part of Emor lists the annual Callings of Holiness—the festivals of the Jewish calendar: the weekly Shabbat; the bringing of the Passover offering on 14 Nisan; the seven-day Passover festival beginning on 15 Nisan; the bringing of the Omer offering from the first barley harvest on the second day of Passover, and the commencement, on that day, of the 49-day Counting of the Omer, culminating in the festival of Shavuot on the fiftieth day; a "remembrance of shofar blowing" on 1 Tishrei; a solemn fast day on 10 Tishrei; the Sukkot festival—during which we are to dwell in huts for seven days and take the "Four Kinds"—beginning on 15 Tishrei; and immediately thereafter, the following holiday of the "eighth day" of Sukkot (Shemini Atzeret).

Next the Torah discusses the lighting of the menorah in the Temple, and the showbread (lechem hapanim) placed weekly on the table there.

Emor concludes with the incident of a man executed for blasphemy, and the penalties for murder (death) and for injuring one's fellow or destroying his property (monetary compensation).

Burial of a *Met Mitzvah*

Priestly Purity

TEXT 1A

Vayikra (Leviticus) 21:1-3

וַיֹּאמֶר ה' אֶל מֹשֶׁה אֱמֹר אֶל הַכֹּהֲנִים בְּנֵי אַהֲרֹן וְאָמַרְתָּ אֲלֵהֶם לְנֶפֶשׁ
לֹא יִטַּמָּא בְּעַמָּיו:
כִּי אִם לִשְׁאֵרוֹ הַקָּרֹב אֵלָיו לְאִמּוֹ וּלְאָבִיו וְלִבְנוֹ וּלְבִתּוֹ וּלְאָחִיו:
וְלַאֲחֹתוֹ הַבְּתוּלָה הַקְּרוֹבָה אֵלָיו אֲשֶׁר לֹא הָיְתָה לְאִישׁ לָהּ יִטַּמָּא:

And G-d said to Moses: Speak to the kohanim, *the sons of Aaron, and say to them: Let none of you defile himself for a dead person among his people.*

Except for his relative who is close to him, his mother, his father, his son, his daughter, his brother.

And for his virgin sister who is close to him, who was not [yet] with a man, for her he shall defile himself.

Another Exception to the Rule

TEXT 1B

Rashi, ad loc.

"לא יטמא בעמיו." בעוד שהמת בתוך עמיו, יצא מת מצוה.

Rabbi Shlomo Yitzchaki
(Rashi)
1040–1105
Most noted biblical and Talmudic commentator. Born in Troyes, France, Rashi studied in the famed *yeshivot* of Mainz and Worms. His commentaries on the Pentateuch and the Talmud, which focus on the straightforward meaning of the text, appear in virtually every edition of the Talmud and Bible.

"Let none of you defile himself for a dead person among his people."

*[This prohibition applies] while the dead person is "among his people" [i.e., he has people, non-*kohanim*, to bury him].*

This comes to exclude [from the prohibition] a met mitzvah, *[a dead person for whom no one is in calling distance to attend to his burial, and thus it is incumbent for people to attend to him].*

What Is the Mitzvah?

TEXT 2A

Maimonides, Sefer Hamitzvot, Mitzvah 231

Rabbi Moshe ben Maimon
(Maimonides, Rambam)
1135–1204

Halachist, philosopher, author, and physician. Maimonides was born in Córdoba, Spain. After the conquest of Córdoba by the Almohads, he fled Spain and eventually settled in Cairo, Egypt. There, he became the leader of the Jewish community and served as court physician to the vizier of Egypt. He is most noted for authoring the *Mishneh Torah*, an encyclopedic arrangement of Jewish law, and for his philosophical work, *Guide for the Perplexed*. His rulings on Jewish law are integral to the formation of halachic consensus.

והמצוה הרל"א היא שצונו לקבור הרוגי בית דין ביום שייהרגו. והוא אמרו יתעלה: "כי קבור תקברנו ביום ההוא". ולשון ספרי: "כי קבור תקברנו מצות עשה". והוא הדין בשאר המתים, כלומר: שייקבר כל מת מישראל ביום מותו.

The 231st mitzvah is that we are commanded to bury those who have been executed by the high court on the same day of their execution. The source of this commandment is the verse "You must certainly bury him on the same day." The Sifri states, "The phrase, 'You must certainly bury him' is a positive commandment."

This law applies to all deceased; every Jew should be buried on the day in which he passes away.

TEXT 2B

Ibid.

ולכן ייקרא המת שאין מי שיתעסק בקבורתו מת מצוה, כלומר: המת שמצוה על כל אדם לקברו לאמרו יתעלה: "קבור תקברנו".

This is the reason why a person who has nobody to arrange his burial is called a met mitzvah. *This means that he is a met [dead person] for whom the mitzvah is on every individual to bury. [The mitzvah referred to is] the verse that states: "You must certainly bury him [on the same day]."*

TEXT 3

Shulchan Aruch, Yoreh Dei'ah 374:3

איזהו מת מצוה, שמצאו בדרך או בעיר של עובדי כוכבים, ואין לו קוברים, וממקום שמצאו אינו יכול לקרות ישראל שיענהו ויבא ליטפל בו ולקוברו, אסור לו לזוז משם ולהניח את המת, אפילו לילך לעיר להביא קוברים, אלא יטמא עצמו ויקברנו.

Rabbi Yosef Caro
(Maran, *Beit Yosef*)
1488–1575

Halachic authority and author. Rabbi Caro was born in Spain, but was forced to flee during the expulsion in 1492 and eventually settled in Safed, Israel. He authored many works including the *Beit Yosef*, *Kesef Mishneh*, and a mystical work, *Magid Meisharim*. Rabbi Caro's magnum opus, the Shulchan Aruch (Code of Jewish Law), has been universally accepted as the basis for modern Jewish law.

What is a met mitzvah? *A body that was found on the road or in a non-Jewish city, and there is nobody to bury it. If there is no Jewish person in the location the body was found who can be called to take care of burial, whoever finds it is forbidden to move from that spot without burying it. It is even forbidden to leave the body in order to travel to call others to bury it. Rather, whoever finds it shall himself become ritually impure and bury it.*

The Nazirite

TEXT 4

Maimonides, Mishneh Torah, Hilchot Nazir 7:12

וכיצד הוא מותר בטומאת מת מצוה, היה מהלך בדרך ופגע במת
שאין שם מי שיקברנו, הרי זה מטמא לו וקוברו. ודברים אלו דברי
קבלה הן.

What is meant by the statement that [a nazir] is permitted to become impure due to contact with a corpse when it is a mitzvah? If he was walking on the road and encountered a corpse and there was no one else to bury it, he should become impure through contact with it and bury it. These matters were communicated by the Oral Tradition.

TEXT 5

Ibid., 7:13

נזיר וכהן שפגעו במת מצוה, יטמא נזיר ואף על פי שהוא סותר הימים הראשונים, ומביא קרבן טומאה, ואל יטמא כהן שזה קדושתו קדושת שעה, ואפילו היה נזיר עולם, והכהן קדושתו קדושת עולם.

When a Nazirite and a priest encounter a corpse that it is a mitzvah [to bury], the Nazirite should [bury it and] become impure, even though he invalidates the days [he observed] previously and must bring a sacrifice [because of his] impurity. The priest should not become impure. [The rationale is that the Nazirite's] holiness is within the context of time—even if he took an everlasting Nazirite vow—while the priest's holiness is beyond the context of time.

Respecting Life— after Death

Human Dignity

TEXT 6

Talmud Tractate Megilah, 3b

Babylonian Talmud

A literary work of monumental proportions that draws upon the legal, spiritual, intellectual, ethical, and historical traditions of Judaism. The 37 tractates of the Babylonian Talmud contain the teachings of the Jewish sages from the period after the destruction of the Second Temple through the fifth century CE. It has served as the primary vehicle for the transmission of the Oral Law and the education of Jews over the centuries; it is the entry point for all subsequent legal, ethical, and theological Jewish scholarship.

תלמוד תורה ומת מצוה מת מצוה עדיף, מדתניא: מבטלין תלמוד תורה להוצאת מת ולהכנסת כלה. עבודה ומת מצוה מת מצוה עדיף . . . בעי רבא: מקרא מגילה ומת מצוה הי מינייהו עדיף? מקרא מגילה עדיף משום פרסומי ניסא, או דלמא מת מצוה עדיף משום כבוד הבריות? בתר דבעיא הדר פשטה: מת מצוה עדיף. דאמר מר: גדול כבוד הבריות שדוחה את לא תעשה שבתורה.

If one must choose between Torah study and tending to a met mitzvah, *the task of burying the* met mitzvah *takes precedence ... Similarly, if one must choose between the Temple service and tending to a* met mitzvah, *tending to the* met mitzvah *takes precedence ... Rava asked: If one must choose between reading the megilah and tending to a* met mitzvah, *which of them takes precedence? Does reading the megilah take precedence due to the value of publicizing the miracle, or perhaps burying the* met mitzvah *takes precedence due to the value of preserving human dignity?*

After he raised the dilemma, Rava then resolved it on his own and ruled that attending to a met mitzvah *takes precedence, as the Master said: Great is human dignity, as it overrides a prohibition in the Torah. [Consequently, it certainly overrides the duty to read the megilah, despite the fact that reading the megilah publicizes the miracle.]*

TEXT 7

Shulchan Aruch, Yoreh De'ah 374:1

מצוה להטמאות למת מצוה, אפילו הוא כהן גדול ונזיר והולך לשחוט את פסחו, ולמול את בנו, ומצא מת מצוה, הרי זה מיטמא לו.

It is a mitzvah to tend to a met mitzvah. *Even a Nazirite high priest on the way to slaughter his Passover offering or to circumcise his son who encounters a* met mitzvah *is obligated to contract ritual impurity by tending to its burial.*

A Worthy Pursuit

TEXT 8

Midrash Vayikra Rabah 34:1

Vayikra Rabah
An early rabbinic commentary on the Book of Leviticus. This Midrash, written in Aramaic and Hebrew, provides textual exegeses and anecdotes, expounds upon the biblical narrative, and develops and illustrates moral principles. It was first printed in Constantinople in 1512 together with four other Midrashic works on the other four books of the Pentateuch.

אשרי משכיל אל דל ביום רעה ימלטהו ה'... רבי יוחנן אמר זה שקובר מת מצוה.

"Praiseworthy is he who looks after the poor; on a day of calamity G-d will rescue him."... Rabbi Yochanan said: This refers to one who buries a met mitzvah.

Right to the Land

TEXT 9

Talmud Tractate Baba Kama, 80b-81a

תנו רבנן: עשרה תנאין התנה יהושע... ומת מצוה קונה מקומו.

The sages taught in a baraita: *Joshua stipulated ten conditions when he apportioned Eretz Yisrael among the tribes... [and the tenth one is:] A* met mitzvah *acquires its place and is buried where it was found.*

TEXT 10

Jerusalem Talmud Tractate Nazir, 7:1

מת מצוה קנה מקומו ארבע אמות אפילו שדה מלא כורכמין, שעל
מנת כן הנחיל יהושע לישראל את הארץ.

A met mitzvah *acquires its place and the surrounding four cubits even in a field full of saffron, for on this condition did Joshua give the Jewish people the land as an inheritance.*

Jerusalem Talmud

A commentary to the Mishnah, compiled during the fourth and fifth centuries. The Jerusalem Talmud predates its Babylonian counterpart by 100 years and is written in both Hebrew and Aramaic. While the Babylonian Talmud is the most authoritative source for Jewish law, the Jerusalem Talmud remains an invaluable source for the spiritual, intellectual, ethical, historical, and legal traditions of Judaism.

Met Mitzvah *in the Diaspora*

TEXT 11

Rabbi Shabetai Hakohen, Shach, Yoreh De'ah 364:10

Rabbi Shabetai ben Meir Hakohen
(Shach)
1621–1662

Also known by the acronym "Shach," after his definitive commentary on Jewish law, *Siftei Kohen*; he was a noted Lithuanian Talmudist and authority on Jewish law. At a very young age, Rabbi Shabetai was appointed to the Vilna Rabbinical Court. *Siftei Kohen*, written when he was 24, is an essential legal commentary on the *Yoreh De'ah* and *Choshen Mishpat* sections of the Shulchan Aruch. When Polish Jewry was devastated by the Chmielnicki Uprisings, Rabbi Shabetai fled to Czechoslovakia.

"וכל המוצאו צריך לקברו במקום שמצאו." ואין צריך להוליכו לקברות וכתב מהרש"ל ומה שהאידנא אין נזהרים בזה הוא לפי שאין הארץ שלנו ואין לנו רשות לקבור בכל מקום ואף אם נקבר אותו לשם יש לחוש שהעובדי כוכבים יחזרו ויוציאו אותו כדי לפשוט בגדיו מעליו [או] משום זלזול ע"כ מוליכין אותו לבית הקברות.

"Whoever finds [a met mitzvah*] must bury it wherever it was found."* He need not bring it to a cemetery. *Maharshal writes that "The reason we don't follow this practice nowadays is that the land we live in does not belong to us and we don't have the authority to bury a* met mitzvah *wherever it may be found. Even if we were to bury it wherever it was found, there is the risk that non-Jews will dig up the grave to remove the corpse's garments or that the grave will be otherwise disrespected. Therefore, we bring the corpse to a cemetery."*

Sweat the Hard Stuff

Met Mitzvot

TEXT 12A

Rabbi Yehudah Hachasid, Sefer Hachasidim, ch. 261

אהוב לך את המצוה הדומה למת מצוה שאין לה עוסקים כגון
שתראה מצוה מבוזיה או תורה שאין לה עוסקים כגון שתראה שבני
עירך לומדים מועד וסדר נשים תלמוד סדר קדשים, ואם תראה
שאין חוששים ללמוד מועד קטן ופרק מי שמתו אתה תלמדם
ותקבל שכר גדול כנגד כולם כי הם דוגמת מת מצוה, אהוב אותן
מסכתות ואותן הלכות שבני אדם אין רגילים בהם.

שזה דומה לאחד שהיו לו בנות ותבעום בני אדם והשיאם להם
ונשארה בת אחת שלא תבעוה לינשא, אמרה לאביה אחיותי
יודעות אומנות נקייה מעשה אורג מעשה רוקם לכך קפצו עליהם
הכל והיו לאנשים אבל למה נתת לי אומנות שהכל מרחיקים ממנה
לארוג בגדי אבל לתכריכי מתים אלו הייתה אומנתי בגדי שמחה
הייתי לאיש כאחת מאחיותי, אמר לה אביה אני משבח אותך
שהכל ילכו אצלך.

כך אמרה מועד קטן והדומה לה רבונו של עולם למה אין עוסקין
בי כשאר מסכתות והקדוש ברוך הוא השיב לה טוב הרי כבר נאמר
"טוב ללכת אל בית אבל מלכת אל בית משתה באשר הוא סוף כל
האדם והחי יתן אל לבו".

Rabbi Yehudah ben Shmuel Hachasid
1140–1217
Mystic and ethicist. Born in Speyer, Germany, he was a rabbi, mystic, and one of the initiators of Chasidei Ashkenaz, a Jewish German moralist movement that stressed piety and asceticism. Rabbi Yehudah settled in Regensburg in 1195. He is best known for his work Sefer Chasidim, on the ethics of day-to-day concerns.

Love a mitzvah that is like a met mitzvah, *i.e., a mitzvah that people don't typically tend to.*

Meaning: If you see a certain mitzvah that is neglected, or that your community regularly studies the Mishnaic orders of Mo'ed *and* Nashim *but neglect to study the Order of* Kodashim, *go and study* Kodashim.

Likewise, if you notice that people don't bother to learn Tractate Moed Katan *and its final chapter* Mi Shemeito *[a chapter dealing with laws of mourning], go and learn them, and you'll be rewarded as though you had learned all the others.*

Such neglected laws and tractates, which are not widely studied, are similar to a met mitzvah, *and one ought to hold them dear.*

By way of analogy, these can be compared to the case of a father who had several daughters, all of whom were married off but for one. She said to her father, "My sisters are expert weavers and embroiderers; therefore, they had many prospective suitors and were easily married. But me you taught the depressing trade of weaving burial shrouds! If only my profession was to create garments for joyous occasions, I'd be married just like my sisters."

Her father replied, "I will praise you highly to all so that you, too, will have many prospective suitors."

In similar fashion, Tractate Moed Katan *and the like say, "Master of the Universe, why am I not studied to the extent that the other tractates are studied?" To which G-d replies, "Doesn't the verse say, 'It is better to go to a house of mourning than to go to a house of feasting, for that is the end of every man, and the living shall lay it to his heart.'"*

TEXT 12B

Sefer Chasidim, ch. 105

כל מצוה שאין לה דורש ואין מי שיבקש אותה תדרשנה לפי שהיא כמת מצוה ומצוה שאין לה רודפים רדוף אחרי' לעשותה שהמצוה מקטרגת ואומרת כמה גרועה אנכי שנתעלמתי מכל וכל.

One ought to promote any mitzvah whose observance is not widely sought after, for such a mitzvah can be likened to a met mitzvah. One ought to pursue the observance of a mitzvah whose observance is not widely pursued, for the mitzvah accuses, as it were, saying, "Look how lowly I am, that I am completely neglected."

No Pain, No Gain

TEXT 13

Mishnah Tractate Avot, 5:21

Mishnah
The first authoritative work of Jewish law that was codified in writing. The Mishnah contains the oral traditions that were passed down from teacher to student; it supplements, clarifies, and systematizes the commandments of the Torah. Due to the continual persecution of the Jewish people, it became increasingly difficult to guarantee that these traditions would not be forgotten. Rabbi Yehudah Hanasi therefore redacted the Mishnah at the end of the second century. It serves as the foundation for the Talmud.

בן הא הא אומר לפום צערא אגרא.

Ben Hei Hei would say: According to the pain is the gain.

Lessons From a Donkey Driver

TEXT 14

Talmud Tractate Chagigah, 9b

אמר ליה בר הי הי להלל מאי דכתיב ושבתם וראיתם בין צדיק
לרשע בין עובד אלהים לאשר לא עבדו היינו צדיק היינו עובד
אלהים היינו רשע היינו אשר לא עבדו אמר ליה עבדו ולא עבדו
תרווייהו צדיקי גמורי נינהו ואינו דומה שונה פרקו מאה פעמים
לשונה פרקו מאה ואחד אמר ליה ומשום חד זימנא קרי ליה לא
עבדו אמר ליה אין צא ולמד משוק של חמרין עשרה פרסי בזוזא
חד עשר פרסי בתרי זוזי.

Bar Hei Hei said to Hillel: What is the meaning of that which is written: "Then you shall again discern … between him who serves G-d and him who does not serve Him"?

Hillel said to him: The one "who serves Him" and the one "who does not serve Him" are both referring to completely righteous people. But the verse is hinting at a distinction between them, as one who reviews his studies one hundred times is not comparable to one who reviews his studies one hundred and one times.

[Bar Hei Hei] said to him: And due to one extra time that he did not review, the verse calls him a person "who does not serve Him"? He said to him: Yes. Go and learn from the market of donkey drivers. One can hire

a driver to travel up to ten parasangs *for one* dinar. *However, he will travel eleven* parasangs *for only two* dinars.

TEXT 15

Rabbi Shneur Zalman of Liadi, Tanya, ch. 15

Rabbi Shneur Zalman of Liadi
(Alter Rebbe)
1745–1812

Chasidic rebbe, halachic authority, and founder of the Chabad movement. The Alter Rebbe was born in Liozna, Belarus, and was among the principal students of the Magid of Mezeritch. His numerous works include the *Tanya*, an early classic containing the fundamentals of Chabad Chasidism, and *Shulchan Aruch HaRav*, an expanded and reworked code of Jewish law.

וּבָזֶה יוּבַן מַה שֶׁכָּתוּב בַּגְּמָרָא, דְּ"עוֹבֵד אֱלֹקִים" הַיְנוּ מִי שֶׁשּׁוֹנֶה פִּרְקוֹ מֵאָה פְעָמִים וְאֶחָד, וְ"לֹא עֲבָדוֹ" הַיְנוּ מִי שֶׁשּׁוֹנֶה פִּרְקוֹ מֵאָה פְעָמִים לְבַד. וְהַיְנוּ מִשּׁוּם שֶׁבִּימֵיהֶם הָיָה הָרְגִילוּת לִשְׁנוֹת כָּל פֶּרֶק מֵאָה פְעָמִים, כִּדְאִיתָא הָתָם בַּגְּמָרָא מָשָׁל מִשּׁוּק שֶׁל חַמָּרִים, שֶׁנִּשְׂכָּרִים לַעֲשָׂר פַּרְסֵי בְּזוּזָא וּלְאַחַד עָשָׂר פַּרְסֵי בִּתְרֵי זוּזֵי, מִפְּנֵי שֶׁהוּא יוֹתֵר מֵרְגִילוּתָם.

וְלָכֵן זֹאת הַפַּעַם הַמֵּאָה וְאַחַת הַיְתֵרָה עַל הָרְגִילוּת שֶׁהֻרְגַּל מִנְּעוּרָיו שְׁקוּלָה כְּנֶגֶד כֻּלָּן, וְעוֹלָה עַל גַּבֵּיהֶן בְּיֶתֶר שְׂאֵת וְיֶתֶר עָז לִהְיוֹת נִקְרָא עוֹבֵד אֱלֹקִים. מִפְּנֵי שֶׁכְּדֵי לְשַׁנּוֹת טֶבַע הָרְגִילוּת, צָרִיךְ לְעוֹרֵר אֶת הָאַהֲבָה לַה', עַל יְדֵי שֶׁמִּתְבּוֹנֵן בִּגְדֻלַּת ה' בְּמֹחוֹ לִשְׁלוֹט עַל הַטֶּבַע שֶׁבֶּחָלָל הַשְּׂמָאלִי הַמָּלֵא דַּם הַנֶּפֶשׁ הַבַּהֲמִית שֶׁמֵּהַקְּלִפָּה, שֶׁמִּמֶּנָּה הוּא הַטֶּבַע. וְזוֹ הִיא עֲבוֹדָה תַּמָּה לַבֵּינוֹנִי. אוֹ לְעוֹרֵר אֶת הָאַהֲבָה הַמְסֻתֶּרֶת שֶׁבְּלִבּוֹ לִמְשֹׁל עַל יָדָהּ עַל הַטֶּבַע שֶׁבֶּחָלָל הַשְּׂמָאלִי, שֶׁזּוֹ נִקְרָא גַּם כֵּן עֲבוֹדָה, לְהִלָּחֵם עִם הַטֶּבַע וְהַיֵּצֶר עַל יְדֵי שֶׁמְּעוֹרֵר הָאַהֲבָה הַמְסֻתֶּרֶת בְּלִבּוֹ. מַה שֶׁאֵין כֵּן כְּשֶׁאֵין לוֹ מִלְחָמָה כְּלָל, אֵין אַהֲבָה זוֹ מִצַּד עַצְמָהּ נִקְרֵאת עֲבוֹדָתוֹ כְּלָל.

This is the meaning of the Talmudic statement that "One who is serving G-d" refers to him who reviews his lesson 101 times, while "One who serves Him not" refers to him who repeats his lesson no more than 100 times. This is because in those days it was customary to review each lesson one hundred times, as the Talmud illustrates with an analogy of a market, where donkey drivers used to hire themselves out at a rate of ten parasangs *for one zuz, but charged two* zuzim *for eleven* parasangs, *because that exceeded their customary practice.*

For the same reason, the 101st review, which is beyond the normal practice a student has been accustomed, since childhood, is considered equivalent to all the previous one hundred times put together, and surpasses them in endurance and effort, earning him the title "one who is serving G-d."

For in order to change his habitual nature, he must arouse the love of G-d by meditating on the greatness of G-d, to gain mastery over the nature of the left part [of the heart], which is full of blood of the animal soul originating in the kelipah, *whence comes his nature. This is a perfect service for a* benoni. *Alternatively, he must awaken the hidden love in his heart to control through it the nature that is in the left part. This, too, is called service—waging a war against his nature and inclination by exciting the love that is hidden in his heart.*

However, if he wages no war at all, the said love in itself can in no way be credited to his service.

The Living Met Mitzvah

TEXT 16

The Lubavitcher Rebbe, Torat Menachem 5744, vol. 3, pp. 1844-1845

Rabbi Menachem Mendel Schneerson
1902–1994

The towering Jewish leader of the 20th century, known as "the Lubavitcher Rebbe," or simply as "the Rebbe." Born in southern Ukraine, the Rebbe escaped Nazi-occupied Europe, arriving in the U.S. in June 1941. The Rebbe inspired and guided the revival of traditional Judaism after the European devastation, impacting virtually every Jewish community the world over. The Rebbe often emphasized that the performance of just one additional good deed could usher in the era of Mashiach. The Rebbe's scholarly talks and writings have been printed in more than 200 volumes.

ישנם יהודים שמסיבות שונות ומשונות הם בבחינת "מת מצוה"... ועל זה אומרים ליהודי, שלמרות שהוא בדרגת "כהן גדול... מכל מקום, מוטלת עליו החובה לרדת ממדרגתו כדי להתעסק עם יהודי שבבחינת "מת מצוה". ובמכ"ש וק"ו: אם כהן גדול צריך לצאת ולהתעסק עם "מת מצוה" כפשוטו, לאחרי שנשמתו נפרדה מגופו, כדי להביאו לתיקונו כו'—הרי על אחת כו"כ שצריך לצאת ולהתעסק עם "מת מצוה" כדי להחיות אותו! וכאמור—מכיון שכהן גדול צריך להניח את העניינים הכי נעלים, עבודת הקטורת ביום הכיפורים בקדש הקדשים, תכלית השלימות בקדושת הכהן גדול, כדי לעסוק עם "מת מצוה", מובן, שעבודה זו חשובה יותר, ומכיון שכן, בהכרח לומר שעל ידה נפעל עילוי גדול יותר אצל הכהן גדול עצמו. וזהו תוכן השליחות של כ"ק מו"ח אדמו"ר נשיא דורנו—שכאו"א צריך לעסוק בהפצת התורה והיהדות והפצת המעיינות בכל מקום שידו מגעת, היינו, לצאת מד' אמות שלו—ד' אמות של תכלית הקדושה—ל"רחוב", כדי לעסוק עם יהודים שהם בבחינת "מת מצוה", ולעשות מהם "לעבעדיקע אידן", יהודים שמקיימים תורה ומצוות.

There are those who, for whatever reason, can be likened to a spiritual met mitzvah ... regarding this a Jew must know, even if you are as lofty as a "high priest" ... nevertheless you are obligated to come down from your spiritual heights to help another Jew who at present is a spiritual met mitzvah. *For if an actual High Priest is obligated to tend to an actual* met mitzvah, *who is no longer physically alive, how much more so must one go out of his way to spiritually revive a living* met mitzvah!

That the High Priest must even put aside his loftiest service in the Temple—the ketoret *on Yom Kippur in the Holy of Holies—for the sake of the* met mitzvah *proves that tending to the* met mitzvah *is more important, and if so it will bring the High Priest to even greater spiritual heights than his Yom Kippur service would.*

This, in short, is the mission taught by my father-in-law, the Rebbe: Each and every one of us must toil in spreading the Torah and Judaism in every place, to leave the four cubits of holiness and go out into the "street," to help those who are like a spiritual met mitzvah *to become* living *Jews who observe the Torah and* mitzvot.

TEXT 17

The Lubavitcher Rebbe, Hayom Yom, Entry for 5 Iyar

רבינו הזקן קבל מרבי מרדכי הצדיק ששמע מהבעל שם טוב: עס
קומט אראפ א נשמה אויף דער וועלט און לעבט אפ זיבעציג אכציג
יאהר, צוליב טאן א אידען א טובה בגשמיות ובפרט אין רוחניות.

The Alter Rebbe received the following teaching from the tzadik Reb Mordechai, who had heard it from the Baal Shem Tov: A soul may descend to this world and live seventy or eighty years—in order to do a Jew a material favor, and certainly a spiritual one.

Appendix

TEXT 18

By Jon Perin

From an e-mail I sent to my family:

I survived my new mitzvah today. It was trying at times, but satisfying. Today, I helped prepare the body of an old man whom I had never met for his funeral.

I wasn't sure how it would go. When I was driving to the mortuary, I couldn't stop asking myself if I would be able to go through with it. I've never been good with doctors. Needles and blood make me feel faint. How would I be able to handle seeing the body of a dead person? In the end, I just decided that I had been asked because there was a need, and therefore I would do it.

I had asked a couple of people for advice the day before. One person told me, "It's the greatest mitzvah, because there's a 100% guarantee that this person will never, ever repay you for the favor you are doing them." I think the thing that finally convinced me was when I found out that if I actually went through with it, I would be the third generation in my family to help in this unique way.

I don't know whether it was intentional or not, but I arrived a little late. The receptionist directed me to the room where the body was being prepared and off I went. I found my way, stuck my head in the doorway, and immediately saw people I knew from shul around a draped body on a table. I took a deep breath, and walked in. I was told how to put on a gown and gloves, shown what brachot to make, and given my job of filling the laver for the person who did the initial washing. No discussions, no opportunity to ask questions, and no chance to back out.

I didn't actually see the body for a few minutes so I just focused my attention on my small job. After a few minutes, my mind seemed to grasp that whatever my fears might have been, there was nothing to worry about.

The thing that initially struck me was how much the physical body changes when the neshamah (soul) is gone. It seems to literally shrink. It was like looking at a balloon the day after a party—slightly shriveled, resting on the floor, a poor reminder of the floating ball of vibrant color you and your kids played with the previous day.

Every time I started to think this way, I was careful to remind myself that this was a man—someone's father, brother, uncle, or husband. At that point, I became more embarrassed about what we were doing than anything else. We did our best to maintain an atmosphere of modesty and kept him covered as much as possible. Conversation during the process was kept to an absolute minimum, mostly just instructions about what to do.

It was so beyond the range of my experience that I didn't know what to expect, and even during the process I still wasn't sure about my own feelings. I just focused on doing what had to be done. There were only a couple of times where a smell would bother me, or seeing how the body reacted after being moved a certain way caught me off guard. By the end of the hour, I was as involved as everyone else there.

It wasn't until after we had dressed him in a shroud and placed him into the casket that it suddenly became familiar to me. The mechanical aspect was done, and it struck me once again that others who knew him would be seeing only the casket. The four of us from the Chevra Kaddisha *(I guess I have to include myself now) were the last to really see him in his current state—a body without a soul. It was truly a sad realization.*

Oddly enough, just yesterday I learned in Talmud that the soul doesn't completely leave the body until the last shovel-full of dirt is placed on the grave. I believe that this is the reason we are so careful as we go through the process of preparing the body. If it feels like someone is watching—it's because someone is, and it's very personal to him or her.

They don't have it easy either. They are experiencing something new and are in a place they have never been before. In many cases, they may be without pain or physical limitations for the first time in a long time.

While I'm sure that it's a welcome relief, I imagine that it's similar to the feeling you have when you are driving and think you might be lost. Do I keep going and hope it turns out okay, or try to turn back and get some help? Unfortunately, turning back is not an option in this case.

As I walked behind the hearse and focused on fulfilling the mitzvah of escorting the dead, I was struck by what I had done. I have been to a number of funerals and been among the mourners. There, everyone focuses on dealing with the living, because that is whom the funeral is truly for. Having been one who focuses on the dead, and after escorting this man as he left the mortuary, I have a new perspective.

I will probably repeat this experience in the future. It was not easy, and I'm sure it won't be next time, but I guess it's not supposed to be. I can't say that I recommend this for everyone. It is mentally, emotionally, and, to a lesser degree, physically challenging. At the same time, it's one of those things that falls into the category of "you have to do it once."

I have more respect than ever for the people of the Chevra Kaddisha and other similar organizations. They have no desire for glory, recognition, fame, or fortune. They don't advertise in newspapers and magazines for support or members. They are most likely the people in your town who are most focused on doing as many mitzvot as possible.

BEHAR-BECHUKOTAI

Kindness Wins

Discipline Is Necessary; Compassion Is Crucial

PARSHAH OVERVIEW
Behar-Bechukotai

On the mountain of Sinai, G-d communicates to Moses the laws of the Sabbatical year: every seventh year, all work on the land should cease, and its produce becomes free for the taking for all, man and beast.

Seven Sabbatical cycles are followed by a fiftieth year—the Jubilee year, on which work on the land ceases, all indentured servants are set free, and all ancestral estates in the Holy Land that have been sold revert to their original owners. Additional laws governing the sale of lands, and the prohibitions against fraud and usury are also given.

G-d promises that if the people of Israel will keep His commandments, they will enjoy material prosperity and dwell securely in their homeland. But He also delivers a harsh "rebuke," warning of the exile, persecution, and other evils that will befall them if they abandon their covenant with Him. Nevertheless, "Even when they are in the land of their enemies, I will not cast them away; nor will I ever abhor them, to destroy them and to break My covenant with them; for I am the L-rd their G-d."

The parshah *concludes with the rules on how to cal-culate the values of different types of pledges made to G-d.*

Shemittah

TEXT 1

Vayikra (Leviticus) 25:1-13

וַיְדַבֵּר ה' אֶל מֹשֶׁה בְּהַר סִינַי לֵאמֹר:

דַּבֵּר אֶל בְּנֵי יִשְׂרָאֵל וְאָמַרְתָּ אֲלֵהֶם כִּי תָבֹאוּ אֶל הָאָרֶץ אֲשֶׁר אֲנִי נֹתֵן
לָכֶם וְשָׁבְתָה הָאָרֶץ שַׁבָּת לַה':

שֵׁשׁ שָׁנִים תִּזְרַע שָׂדֶךָ וְשֵׁשׁ שָׁנִים תִּזְמֹר כַּרְמֶךָ וְאָסַפְתָּ אֶת תְּבוּאָתָהּ:

וּבַשָּׁנָה הַשְּׁבִיעִת שַׁבַּת שַׁבָּתוֹן יִהְיֶה לָאָרֶץ שַׁבָּת לַה' שָׂדְךָ לֹא תִזְרָע
וְכַרְמְךָ לֹא תִזְמֹר:...

וְסָפַרְתָּ לְךָ שֶׁבַע שַׁבְּתֹת שָׁנִים שֶׁבַע שָׁנִים שֶׁבַע פְּעָמִים וְהָיוּ לְךָ יְמֵי
שֶׁבַע שַׁבְּתֹת הַשָּׁנִים תֵּשַׁע וְאַרְבָּעִים שָׁנָה:

וְהַעֲבַרְתָּ שׁוֹפַר תְּרוּעָה בַּחֹדֶשׁ הַשְּׁבִעִי בֶּעָשׂוֹר לַחֹדֶשׁ בְּיוֹם הַכִּפֻּרִים
תַּעֲבִירוּ שׁוֹפָר בְּכָל אַרְצְכֶם:

וְקִדַּשְׁתֶּם אֵת שְׁנַת הַחֲמִשִּׁים שָׁנָה וּקְרָאתֶם דְּרוֹר בָּאָרֶץ לְכָל
יֹשְׁבֶיהָ יוֹבֵל הִוא תִּהְיֶה לָכֶם וְשַׁבְתֶּם אִישׁ אֶל אֲחֻזָּתוֹ וְאִישׁ אֶל
מִשְׁפַּחְתּוֹ תָּשֻׁבוּ:

יוֹבֵל הִוא שְׁנַת הַחֲמִשִּׁים שָׁנָה תִּהְיֶה לָכֶם לֹא תִזְרָעוּ וְלֹא תִקְצְרוּ אֶת
סְפִיחֶיהָ וְלֹא תִבְצְרוּ אֶת נְזִרֶיהָ:

כִּי יוֹבֵל הִוא קֹדֶשׁ תִּהְיֶה לָכֶם מִן הַשָּׂדֶה תֹּאכְלוּ אֶת תְּבוּאָתָהּ:

בִּשְׁנַת הַיּוֹבֵל הַזֹּאת תָּשֻׁבוּ אִישׁ אֶל אֲחֻזָּתוֹ:

And G-d spoke to Moses on Mount Sinai, saying:

"Speak to the Children of Israel and you shall say to them: When you come to the land that I am giving

you, the land shall rest [for one year in every seven; it is] a Sabbath to G-d.

"You may sow your field for six years, and for six years you may prune your vineyard and gather in its produce,

"But in the seventh year, the land shall have a complete rest, a Sabbath to G-d; you shall not sow your field, nor shall you prune your vineyard ...

"And you shall count for yourself seven sabbatical years, seven years seven times. And the days of these seven sabbatical years shall amount to forty-nine years for you.

"You shall proclaim [with] the shofar blasts, in the seventh month, on the tenth of the month; on the Day of Atonement, you shall sound the shofar throughout your land.

"And you shall sanctify the fiftieth year, and proclaim freedom [for slaves] throughout the land for all who live on it. It shall be a Jubilee for you, and you shall return, each man to his property, and you shall return, each man to his family.

"This fiftieth year shall be a Jubilee for you; you shall not sow, nor shall you reap its aftergrowth or pick [its grapes] that you had set aside [for yourself].

"For it is Jubilee. It shall be holy for you; you shall eat its produce from the field.

"During this Jubilee year, you shall return, each man to his property."

Origins

TEXT 2

Rashi, ad loc.

Rabbi Shlomo Yitzchaki
(Rashi)
1040–1105
Most noted biblical and
Talmudic commentator.
Born in Troyes, France,
Rashi studied in the famed
yeshivot of Mainz and
Worms. His commentaries
on the Pentateuch and
the Talmud, which focus
on the straightforward
meaning of the text, appear
in virtually every edition
of the Talmud and Bible.

"בהר סיני". מה ענין שמיטה אצל הר סיני, והלא כל המצות נאמרו
מסיני? אלא מה שמיטה נאמרו כללותיה ופרטותיה ודקדוקיה
מסיני, אף כולן נאמרו כללותיהן ודקדוקיהן מסיני, כך שנויה
בתורת כהנים.

ונראה לי שכך פירושה לפי שלא מצינו שמיטת קרקעות שנשנית
בערבות מואב במשנה תורה, למדנו שכללותיה ופרטותיה כולן
נאמרו מסיני, ובא הכתוב ולמד כאן על כל דבור שנדבר למשה
שמסיני היו כולם כללותיהן ודקדוקיהן, וחזרו ונשנו בערבות מואב.

"On Mount Sinai:" What [special relevance] does the subject of **Shemittah** have with Mount Sinai? Were not all the commandments stated from Sinai? However, [this teaches us that] just as with Shemittah, *its general principles and its finer details were all stated from Sinai,* likewise, all of them were stated—their gen-

eral principles [together with] their finer details—from Sinai. This is what is taught in Torat Kohanim.

[And why is Shemittah *used as the example to prove this rule?] I would suggest as follows: [At the plains of Moab, Moses reiterated the majority of the laws of the Torah to the Israelites before their entry into the Land of Israel; this reiteration comprises most of the Book of Deuteronomy. Now,] since we do not find the laws of* Shemittah *["release"] of land reiterated on the plains of Moab in Deuteronomy, we learn that its general principles, finer details, and explanations were all stated at Sinai. Scripture states this [phrase] here to teach us that [just as in the case of* Shemittah,*] every statement [i.e., every commandment] that was conveyed to Moses came from Sinai, [including] their general principles and finer details [and that the commandments delineated in Deuteronomy were merely] repeated and reviewed on the plains of Moab [not originally given there].*

The Paradox of Shemittah

A Year of Faith

TEXT 3

Talmud Tractate Sanhedrin, 39a

Babylonian Talmud

A literary work of monumental proportions that draws upon the legal, spiritual, intellectual, ethical, and historical traditions of Judaism. The 37 tractates of the Babylonian Talmud contain the teachings of the Jewish sages from the period after the destruction of the Second Temple through the fifth century CE. It has served as the primary vehicle for the transmission of the Oral Law and the education of Jews over the centuries; it is the entry point for all subsequent legal, ethical, and theological Jewish scholarship.

אתא ההוא תלמידא אמר ליה מאי טעמא דשביעתא? אמר ליה
... אמר הקדוש ברוך הוא לישראל זרעו שש והשמיטו שבע כדי
שתדעו שהארץ שלי היא והן לא עשו כן אלא חטאו וגלו.
(רש"י: כדי שתדעו וכו' - ולא ירום לבבכם בשבח ארצכם ותשכחו
עול מלכותו.)

A disciple came and asked [Rabbi Abbahu], "What is the reason for the Sabbatical year?"

Rabbi Abbahu replied … The Holy One, blessed be He, said to Israel, "Sow your seed six years, but omit the seventh, so that you may know that the earth is Mine." They, however, did not do so, but sinned and were exiled.

(Rashi: "So that you may know, etc."—And your heart will not grow arrogant over the produce of your land and forget the yoke of His Kingship.)

Trust Me

TEXT 4

Rabbi Aharon Halevi of Barcelona, Sefer Hachinuch, Mitzvah 84

Sefer Hachinuch

A work on the biblical commandments. Four aspects of every mitzvah are discussed in this work: the definition of the mitzvah; ethical lessons that can be deduced from the mitzvah; basic laws pertaining to the observance of the mitzvah; and who is obligated to perform the mitzvah, and when. The work was composed in the 13th century by an anonymous author who refers to himself as "the Levite of Barcelona." It has been widely thought that this referred to Rabbi Aharon Halevi of Barcelona (Re'ah); however, this view has been contested.

משרשי המצוה, לקבוע בלבנו ולצייר ציור חזק במחשבתנו ענין חדוש העולם כי ששת ימים עשה ה' את השמים ואת הארץ, וביום השביעי שלא ברא דבר הכתיב מנוחה על עצמו. ולמען הסיר ולעקור ולשרש מרעיונינו דבר הקדמות אשר יאמינו הכופרים בתורה ובו יהרסו כל פנותיה ויפרצו חומותיה, באה חובה עלינו להוציא כל זמנינו יום יום ושנה שנה על דבר זה למנות שש שנים ולשבות בשביעית, ובכן לא יתפרד הענין לעולם מבין עינינו תמיד, והוא כענין שאנו מוציאין ימי השבוע בששת ימי עבודה ויום מנוחה. ולכן ציוה ברוך הוא להפקיר כל מה שתוציא הארץ בשנה זו מלבד השביתה בה, כדי שיזכור האדם כי הארץ שמוציאה אליו הפירות בכל שנה ושנה לא בכוחה וסגולתה תוציא אותם . . .

ועוד יש תועלת אחר נמצא בזה האדם שיוסיף האדם בטחון בשם ברוך הוא, כי כל המוצא עם לבבו לתת ולהפקיר לעולם כל גדולי קרקעותיו ונחלת אבותיו הגדלים בכל שנה אחת, ומלומד בכך הוא וכל המשפחה כל ימיו, לא תחזק בו לעולם מדת הכילות הרבה ולא מיעוט הבטחון.

The purpose of this mitzvah is to affix the notion that G-d created the world in our hearts and minds, the matter of the world having been created. As the verses states, "In six days did G-d make the heavens and the earth, and on the seventh day," in which He did not create anything, He imposed rest on Himself.

This mitzvah serves to remove, uproot, and eradicate from our minds the notion that the world was always extant, [i.e., that it was not created, but always was], a belief held by those who deny the Torah and seek to destroy all its principles and break through its walls. So, we are commanded to dedicate time, day by day and year by year, for this matter, by counting six years and resting on the seventh, so that this matter will never depart from between our eyes for all time. This whole process is similar to how we count the days of the week—dividing them into six days of work and a seventh day of rest.

For this reason, in addition to resting during this year, G-d, blessed be He, commanded us to render all produce of the land as ownerless. The purpose of this is so that a person will remember that the land that produces fruits for him every year does so not by its might and virtue. ...

And there is another benefit; the outcome of this is that a person will add to his trust in G-d, may He be blessed, because anyone who finds it in his heart to give and abandon to the world all of the produce of his lands and his ancestral inheritance for an entire year, and educates himself and his family through this for all of his days, will never have the trait of stinginess overcome him too much, nor will he have a deficient amount of trust.

TEXT 5

The Lubavitcher Rebbe, Likutei Sichot, vol. 1, p. 274

Rabbi Menachem Mendel Schneerson
1902–1994

The towering Jewish leader of the 20th century, known as "the Lubavitcher Rebbe," or simply as "the Rebbe." Born in southern Ukraine, the Rebbe escaped Nazi-occupied Europe, arriving in the U.S. in June 1941. The Rebbe inspired and guided the revival of traditional Judaism after the European devastation, impacting virtually every Jewish community the world over. The Rebbe often emphasized that the performance of just one additional good deed could usher in the era of Mashiach. The Rebbe's scholarly talks and writings have been printed in more than 200 volumes.

דער ענין פון שמיטה כפשוטו איז, אז בשנה השביעית דארף זיין שבתון לארץ שדך לא תזרע וכרמך לא תזמור וגו'. בשנה השביעית דארף זיין שביתה אין די אלע ענינים פון מלאכות הארץ פון וואס מען מאכט לחם וכו' שעליו יחיה האדם.

וכי תאמרו מה נאכל? אויף דעם ענטפערט די תורה, וצויתי את ברכתי גו' ועשת את התבואה לשלש השנים.

דער תוכן פון דעם ענין פון מצות שמיטה איז: מען מאנט ביי א אידן אז איין מאל אין זיבן יאר זאל ער זיך זעגענען פון אלע ענינים ארציים, ערדישע באדערפענישין, ער זאל ניט האבן צו טאן מיט מלאכות הארץ וואס זיינען פארבונדן מיט דעם לחם שעליו יחיה האדם, און ער זאל זיך אינגאנצן פארלאזן אויף דעם אויבערשטן, אז ער וועט אים געבן זיין פרנסה למעלה מהטבע.

The plain sense of Shemittah *is that the land must rest in the seventh year, "You shall not sow your field, nor shall you prune your vineyard." In the seventh year, one must suspend all forms of work in the fields that produce the staple food by which man lives.*

"And if you should say: What shall we eat?" The Torah answers, "[Know, then, that] I will command My blessing for you in the sixth year… and it will yield produce for three years."

Thus, the underlying concept of Shemittah *is that once in every seven years a Jew is expected to divest from all mundane needs. A person is to disengage from all involvements with the land that would yield the bread that is his or her sustenance. [Rather], they depend completely on G-d, that He will provide sustenance beyond the natural way.*

Mankind's Purpose

TEXT 6

Rabbi Yitzchak Arama, Akeidat Yitzchak, ch. 69

Rabbi Yitzchak Arama
1420–1494
Spanish rabbi and philosopher; known as "the Baal Akeidah," after his work, *Akeidat Yitzchak*, an influential philosophic and mystical commentary on the Torah. After initially serving as head of the yeshivah in Zamora, Spain, he was appointed as rabbi and preacher for the community of Tarragona. His writings were received favorably by his peers, including Rabbi Don Yitzchak Abarbanel. After the expulsion of 1492, Rabbi Arama ultimately settled in Naples, where he is buried.

וזה כי במספר שבע שני העבודה ושביתת השביעיות העיר את לבנו
והשמיע לאזנינו כי לא שולחנו הנה להיות עבדים נמכרים לאדמה
כי אם לתכלית אחר נכבד ונפלא ממנו ושלא נתכוין בעבודתה
רק לכדי צורך אוכל נפש ושאר הספוקים בעוד שאנו משתדלים
בהשגת התכלית ההוא העליון כמו שכתבנו בפרק שביעי מהשער
הנזכר וזאת היא כוונת מתנת הארץ הזאת אל זאת האומ' כמו
שאמרנו ראשונה . . . הכוונה שכניסתן לארץ אינה להשתעבד לה
ולעבודתה להוציא פירותיה ולאצור פירותיה לקבוץ אותם על
יד כדי להתעשר בהם כמו שהיא כוונת שאר העמים בארצותם
כמו שאמר "וישבו בארץ ויסחרו אותה והארץ הנה רחבת ידים
לפניהם". **רק הכוונה כדי שיעמדו על עצמן וידרשו שלמותם כפי
רצון בוראם.**

Through counting seven [Shemittah cycles: six] years of work and the seventh of rest, [the Torah informed us] that we were not sent [to this world] to be servants of the land. Rather for a different purpose, one more

honorable and wondrous [is man's purpose], and work-
ing the land is intended only in order to feed ourselves
and acquire other needs so that we can achieve that
higher purpose ... This is the intention of the gift of the
land to this nation, as stated here previously ... The
purpose of the Jewish people's entering the land was
not to be servants of the land, to work it for its produce
[to simply amass wealth]; rather, the intention was
only so that they would be able to sustain themselves
and live peacefully, according the will of their Creator.

TEXT 7

Rabbi Avraham ibn Ezra, Ibn Ezra to Shemot 20:8

Rabbi Avraham ibn Ezra
1092–1167

Biblical commentator, linguist, and poet. Ibn Ezra was born in Toledo, Spain and fled the Almohad regime to other parts of Europe. It is believed that he was living in London at the time of his death. Ibn Ezra is best known for his literalistic commentary on the Pentateuch. He also wrote works of poetry, philosophy, medicine, astronomy, and other topics.

ראינו כי שנת השמטה דומה לשבת כי גם היא שביעית בשניה. וצוה השם שיקראו התורה בתחלת השנה נגד האנשים והנשים והטף ואמר הטעם למען ישמעו ולמען ילמדו ושמרו. והנה השבת נתנה להבין מעשה השם ולהגות בתורתו. וככה כתוב כי שמחתני ה' בפעליך. כל ימי השבוע אדם מתעסק בצרכיו. והנה זה היום ראוי להתבודד ולשבות בעבור כבוד השם.

The year of Shemittah is similar to Shabbat, because it is also the seventh in yearly cycles. G-d commanded that the Torah should be read publicly at the beginning of a [Shemittah] year before all men, women, and children, so that they should hear, learn, and observe [the Torah.] [Similarly,] Shabbat was given so that we may understand the deeds of G-d and study His Torah. This is what is written in the verse "For I rejoice in G-d's deeds." During the weekdays a person should deal with his needs. But on [Shabbat] it is fitting to meditate in solitude and rest for the sake of G-d.

Combined Forces

TEXT 8

Likutei Sichot, Ibid.

א סדר אויף אלע מאל איז עס ניט. רוב הזמן—בכמות—דארף
א איד האבן צו טאן מיט עניני העולם, צוליב עבודת הבירורים.
דאס איז דאך דער ענין וואס התהוות העולם איז געווען דורכן שם
אלקים בגימטריא הטבע, בכדי דער אדם זאל זיך עוסק זיין על פי
תורה אין די ענינים פון טבע, און דורך דעם מברר ומזכך זיין די
עניני הטבע.

אבער אין געוויסע צייטן, מאנט מען ביים אידן, ער זאל ארויס פון
וועלט, הגם מען דארף איר טאקע מברר זיין. אבער בזמן מן הזמנים
דארף זיין די תנועה, צו שטעלן זיך העכער פון וועלט.

די די צווי ענינים זיינען אפהענגיק איינער פון צווייטן.

בכדי עס זאל זיין די תנועה פון שטעלן זיך העכער פון וועלט . . .
איז דאס דורך דעם וואס האבנדיק צו טאן מיט עניני העולם איז
עס על פי תורה.

This approach [of transcending the world completely], however, is not meant to be the norm. Most of the time—quantitatively speaking—a Jew must be involved with mundane matters for the purpose of refining the physical world. That is why the world was created with the divine name Elokim, the numerical value of which is the same as "hateva (nature)." For man must relate to things as they are in the natural order in the way prescribed for him in the Torah, and thereby he purifies and refines those things of nature.

On the other hand, there are certain times when a Jew is enjoined to step out of the world. To be sure, the world must be purified. Nonetheless, at certain times, there must be a move toward placing oneself beyond— higher than—the world.

These two approaches actually hinge upon each other: In order to successfully maintain an attitude that transcends the world, the level of engagement a person does *have with the world must be dictated by the Torah.*

The Prototypical Mitzvah

TEXT 9

Ibid.

לויט דעם וועט מען אויך פארשטיין וואס מצות שמיטה איז א
מצוה כללית; דאס איז דער תוכן פון אלע מצות. נאר אין מצות
שמיטה איז דאס בגילוי.

דער אלטער רבי דערקלערט אין תניא אז דער עסק אין תורה
ומצות און תפלה, איז אן ענין פון מסירת נפש ממש כמו בצאתה
מן הגוף כו׳ שאינה מהרהרת בצרכי הגוף אלא מחשבתה מיוחדת
ומלובשת באותיות התורה והתפלה. דאס הייסט אז בשעת עסק
התורה ומצות ותפלה דארף זיין דער הרגש פונקט ווי ער איז שוין
נאך יציאת הנפש מהגוף, אליך הוי׳ נפשי אשא.

פון דער צווייטער זייט, מאנט מען ביי אים, אז יעדער מצוה זאל
ער מקיים זיין כתיקונה, מיט אירע הגבלות אין זמן און מקום און
מיט אלע דקדוקים וואס אין יעדער מצוה, וואס דאס זיינען דאך
הגבלות פון וועלט.

דאס הייסט אז דער ענין פון מצות איז: מען דארף נעמען די תנועה
פון מסירת נפש, אויסגעטאן פון גוף און גשמיות, און מיט דער
תנועה גופא מקיים זיין די מצוה בכל פרטיה ודקדוקיה: המשכת
בלי-גבול בגבול.

נאר אין סתם מצות איז דאס פארבארגן, דאס הערט זיך נאר אן אין
דעם אופן קיום המצות. אבער ביי שמיטה איז דאס בגלוי און עס
הערט זיך אן אין דער מצוה אליין.

All this explains how the mitzvah of Shemittah *is a prototypical mitzvah. Its message is the very essence of all* mitzvot, *and in the mitzvah of* Shemittah *it is expressed explicitly.*

The Alter Rebbe explains in Tanya *that, "Involvement with Torah,* mitzvot *and prayer is a matter of actual* mesirat nefesh *(surrender of the soul), as when (the soul) leaves the body… for it no longer thinks of bodily needs; it is as though it is united with and vested in the letters of Torah and prayer." This means the when involved with Torah,* mitzvot *and prayer, one must feel just as after the soul has already left the body—"Unto You, G-d, I lift up my soul."*

Contrarily, one must also observe every mitzvah precisely as prescribed, with all the stipulations related to time and place, and all the specific details of every mitzvah. All these stipulations and details are restrictions and limitations related to the reality of the physical world.

The divine commandments, then, contain two elements: a) There must be an approach of mesirat nefesh, *divesture from the body and physical reality; and b) in that very same frame of mind one must observe the mitzvah in all its details and specifications. The finite is thus infused with infinity.*

With mitzvot *in general, this requirement is concealed. It becomes notable only in the way they are observed. With the mitzvah of* Shemittah, *however, it is explicit. It is notable in that mitzvah itself.*

The Yovel Paradox

Strong Humility

TEXT 10

Sefer Hachinuch, Mitzvah 330

משרשי המצוה. על צד הפשט, שרצה השם יתברך להודיע לעמו
כי הכל שלו, ולבסוף ישוב כל דבר לאשר חפץ הוא לתנה בתחלה,
כי לו הארץ, כמו שכתוב "כי לי כל הארץ".

A simple perspective on the purpose of the mitzvah of Yovel is that G-d, may He be blessed, wanted to inform His nation that everything is His; and in the end everything will return to those to whom He wanted to give it at first—for the earth is His, as it is stated, "for all the earth is Mine."

TEXT 11

The Lubavitcher Rebbe, Hayom Yom, Entry for 4 Menachem Av

מיט דער גרעסטער הארעוואניע קען מען ניט פארדינען קיין איין
סענט מעהר וויפיל השם יתברך האט אפגעשטעלט, אז דער און
דער מענש זאל פארדינען. מען בעדארף טאן וויפיל עס איז נויטיג,
אבער מען מוז געדיינקען, אז די גאנצע ארבעט, איז מער ניט ווי
א טפל, דער עיקר איז די ברכה פון השם יתברך, און די ברכה
פארדינט מען ווען מען איז א ערליכער איד: תפלה בצבור, שמירת
שבת בהידור כשרות בהשגחה גדולה, חינוך הבנים בא מלמדים
ערליכע אידען.

*No matter how much effort is exerted, it is impossible
to earn even one cent more than what G-d has destined
that this particular person shall earn. A person must
do what is necessary, but he or she must remember
that all his or her work is but an adjunct. The main
thing is G-d's blessing, and that blessing is earned by
being observant of G-d's commands:* Davening *with
a minyan,* observing Shabbat *b'hidur (beyond the
minimum, with "beauty"), meticulous observance of*
kashrut, *and educating children with upright teachers.*

Strong Pride

TEXT 12

Rabbi Levi ben Gershon, Pirush Haralbag to Vayikra, ch. 25

והנה בענין שוב האחוזה לבעליה ביובל, ושוב האדם למשפחתו,
תועלת אחר; והוא, כי זה יהיה סיבה שלא יהיו נואשים מטוב,
האנשים הקשי-יום, לדעתם כי בבוא היובל ישובו אל קניניהם,
ולזה יהיה להם חריצות להשתדל לאסוף ולכנוס מה שיצטרך להם
למחיתם, ולא יתרשלו ותרפינה ידיהם לחושבם שאין להם תקומה
עוד, כמו שתראה בקצת האנשים שהם נואשים מטוב לזאת הסיבה,
והיה זה סיבה אל התמדת חסרונם.

There is another purpose to the law that property returns to its original owner and slaves are freed during the Yovel. The idea is that people who endure daily hardship should never lose hope, armed with the knowledge that they will one day be set free. In this manner, they will be motivated to persist in their efforts to do everything to stay alive and well, not despairing under the assumption that they have no hope. Indeed, we observe such conduct with people found in such desperate situations—their enduring slavery is the reason for their persistent disadvantage.

Conclusion—The Mountain: Pride or Humility

TEXT 13

Targum Yonatan ben Uziel to Shoftim 5:5

Yonatan ben Uziel
ca. First Century CE
Considered by the Talmud
to be Hillel the Elder's most
distinguished pupil; author
of the *Targum Yonatan*, a
comprehensive Aramaic
translation of the Prophets.
In Talmudic times, *Targum
Yonatan* was read in the
synagogue as a verse-by-verse
translation of the Hebrew
haftarah. Little is known about
his personal life. In recent
years, his tomb, in Amukah
in the Galilee, has become a
popular place of pilgrimage.

טוּרַיָא זָעוּ מִן קֳדָם יְיָ טוּרָא דְתָבוֹר טוּרָא דְחֶרְמוֹן וְטוּרָא דְכַרְמְלָא
מִתְרַגְשִׁין דֵין עִם דֵין וְאָמְרִין דֵין לְדֵין דֵין אֲמַר עֲלַי תִּשְׁרֵי שְׁכִנְתֵּיה
וְלִי חֲזֵיָא וְדֵין לְדֵין אֲמַר עֲלַי תִּשְׁרֵי שְׁכִנְתֵּיה וְלִי חֲזֵיָא אַשְׁרֵי שְׁכִנְתֵּיה
עַל טוּרָא דְסִינַי דְהוּא חַלָשׁ וּזְעֵיר מִכָּל טוּרַיָא.

"The mountains trembled before G-d." Mounts Tabor, Hermon, and Carmel were quarrelling with one another, claiming, "I am most befitting to be the host of G-d's glory; surely He will bestow His grace on me!"

G-d, however, bestowed His glory upon Mount Sinai, which is more humble and meeker than all other mountains.

6

SHAVUOT

Three Is the Magic Number

Achieving Harmony in the Face of Controversy

PARSHAH OVERVIEW
Shavuot

On the first day of Shavuot we read from Exodus, chapters 19 and 20.

A summary of the content: The Children of Israel camp opposite Mount Sinai, where they are told that G-d has chosen them to be His "kingdom of priests" and "holy nation." The people respond by proclaiming, "All that G-d has spoken, we shall do."

On the sixth day of the third month (Sivan), seven weeks after the Exodus, the entire nation of Israel assembles at the foot of Mount Sinai. G-d descends on the mountain amidst thunder, lightning, billows of smoke, and the blast of the shofar, and summons Moses to ascend.

G-d proclaims the Ten Commandments, commanding the people of Israel to believe in G-d, not to worship idols or take G-d's name in vain, to honor their parents, keep the Shabbat, and not to murder, commit adultery, steal, bear false witness, or covet another's property. The people cry out to Moses that the revelation is too intense for them to bear, begging him to receive the Torah from G-d and convey it to them.

On the second day of Shavuot, we read from Deuteronomy, chapters 14-16, which detail the laws of the three pilgrimage festivals—Passover, Shavuot, and Sukkot—on which all Jews came "to see and be seen before the face of G-d" in the Holy Temple in Jerusalem.

A Story about Three

The Torah Is Given

TEXT 1

Shemot (Exodus) 19:1

בַּחֹדֶשׁ הַשְּׁלִישִׁי לְצֵאת בְּנֵי יִשְׂרָאֵל מֵאֶרֶץ מִצְרָיִם בַּיּוֹם הַזֶּה בָּאוּ
מִדְבַּר סִינָי:

*In the third month of the Children of Israel's departure
from Egypt, on this day they arrived in the desert
of Sinai.*

TEXT 2A

Babylonian Talmud
A literary work of monumental
proportions that draws upon
the legal, spiritual, intellectual,
ethical, and historical
traditions of Judaism. The 37
tractates of the Babylonian
Talmud contain the teachings
of the Jewish sages from the
period after the destruction
of the Second Temple through
the fifth century CE. It has
served as the primary vehicle
for the transmission of the
Oral Law and the education
of Jews over the centuries;
it is the entry point for all
subsequent legal, ethical, and
theological Jewish scholarship.

Talmud Tractate Shabbat, 88a

דרש ההוא גלילאה עליה דרב חסדא: בריך רחמנא דיהב אוריאן
תליתאי לעם תליתאי, על ידי תליתאי, ביום תליתאי, בירחא תליתאי.

*A scholar taught the following in the yeshiva of Rav
Chisda: "Blessed is the Merciful One who gave a three-
part Torah to a three-part [Jewish] nation, through
[Moses who was] the third [child in his family], on the*

third day, in the third month (i.e., the Hebrew month of Sivan)."

TEXT 2B

Rashi, ad loc.

"אוריאן תליתאי". תורה נביאים וכתובים.

"לעם תליתאי". כהנים לוים וישראלים.

"על יד תליתאי". משה תליתאי לבטן, מרים אהרן ומשה.

"ביום תליתאי". לפרישה.

Rabbi Shlomo Yitzchaki (Rashi)
1040–1105
Most noted biblical and Talmudic commentator. Born in Troyes, France, Rashi studied in the famed *yeshivot* of Mainz and Worms. His commentaries on the Pentateuch and the Talmud, which focus on the straightforward meaning of the text, appear in virtually every edition of the Talmud and Bible.

"A three-part Torah." [Namely,] the Five Books of Moses, the Books of the Prophets, and the Scriptural Writings.

"To a three-part nation." Comprised of three groups, Kohanim, Leviim, and Yisraelim.

"Through the third." Moses was the third child; his older siblings were Miriam and Aaron.

"On the third day." The third day of preparation for the receiving of the Torah.

A Three-Part Teaching Method

TEXT 3

Midrash Torat Kohanim, Parshat Vayikra

רבי ישמעאל אומר בשלש עשרה מדות התורה נדרשת... וכן
שני כתובין המכחישים זה את זה עד שיבא הכתוב השלישי
ויכריע ביניהם.

*Rabbi Yishmael says, "The Torah is interpreted
through thirteen different pedagogic methods … #13:
When two scriptural verses contradict each other, a
third verse will come to reconcile them."*

Sample 1: The Sinai Narrative

TEXT 4A

Shemot (Exodus) 20:18

וַיֹּאמֶר ה' אֶל מֹשֶׁה כֹּה תֹאמַר אֶל בְּנֵי יִשְׂרָאֵל אַתֶּם רְאִיתֶם כִּי מִן
הַשָּׁמַיִם דִּבַּרְתִּי עִמָּכֶם:

*G-d said to Moses, "So shall you say to the Children
of Israel, You have seen that from the heavens I have
spoken with you.*

TEXT 4B

Rashi, Ibid.

"כי מן השמים דברתי". וכתוב אחד אומר "וירד ה' על הר סיני",
בא הכתוב השלישי והכריע ביניהם: "מן השמים השמיעך את קולו
ליסרך ועל הארץ הראך את אשו הגדולה", כבודו בשמים ואשו
וגבורתו על הארץ.
דבר אחר הרכין שמים ושמי השמים והציען על ההר, וכן הוא אומר
"ויט שמים וירד".

*"From the heavens I have spoken." But another verse
states, "G-d descended upon Mount Sinai" [implying
that G-d spoke from the mountain, not the heavens]?*

*A third verse comes and reconciles them, "From the
heavens He let you hear His voice in order to discipline you, and upon the earth He displayed His great
fire"—His glory is in the heavens, and His fire is upon
the earth.*

*Alternatively, He bent down the [lower] heavens
and the highest heavens and spread them out upon
the mountain. So [Scripture] says, "And He bent the
heavens, and He came down."*

Sample 2: The Tabernacle

TEXT 5A

Bamidbar (Numbers) 7:89

וּבְבֹא מֹשֶׁה אֶל אֹהֶל מוֹעֵד לְדַבֵּר אִתּוֹ וַיִּשְׁמַע אֶת הַקּוֹל מִדַּבֵּר אֵלָיו מֵעַל הַכַּפֹּרֶת אֲשֶׁר עַל אֲרֹן הָעֵדֻת מִבֵּין שְׁנֵי הַכְּרֻבִים וַיְדַבֵּר אֵלָיו:

When Moses would enter the Tent of Meeting to speak with [G-d], he would hear [G-d's] voice speaking to him from the two cherubim above the covering that was placed on the Ark of Testimony [in the Holy of Holies], and He spoke to him.

TEXT 5B

Rashi, Ibid.

"ובבא משה". שני כתובים המכחישים זה את זה, בא שלישי והכריע ביניהם. כתוב אחד אומר "וידבר ה' אליו מאהל מועד" והוא חוץ לפרכת, וכתוב אחד אומר "ודברתי אתך מעל הכפרת" בא זה והכריע ביניהם משה בא אל אהל מועד ושם שומע את הקול הבא מעל הכפרת.

"When Moses would enter." [When there are] two contradictory verses, the third one comes and reconciles them. One verse says, "G-d spoke to him from

the Tent of Meeting," and that implies outside the curtain, [within the Sanctuary,] whereas another verse says, "And speak to you from above the ark cover," [which is beyond the curtain, in the Holy of Holies]. This [third verse] comes and reconciles them: [When] Moses would enter the Tent of Meeting, he would hear the voice [of G-d] coming from [Holy of Holies, from between the cherubim,] above the ark cover. . . . The voice emanated from heaven to [the area] between the two cherubim, and from there it went out to the Tent of Meeting.

TEXT 6

The Lubavitcher Rebbe, Sefer Hasichot 5749, vol. 2, p. 510

לכאורה אינו מובן: למה נכתב הענין בתורה באופן שלכתחילה ישנם שני כתובים **המכחישים** זה את זה, "הכשה" על פי תורת אמת, ואחר כך ניתוסף "כתוב השלישי" **שמכריע ביניהם**—הרי התורה היתה יכולה לכתוב לכתחילה מסקנת הענין שבכתוב השלישי?!

It is puzzling: Why does the Torah write things in a way that first we have two contradictory verses—a legitimate, Torah-sanctioned "contradiction," mind you—and only afterwards do we arrive at the third verse which reconciles the matter? Couldn't the Torah have simply written the conclusion as it is in the third verse to begin with?

Rabbi Menachem Mendel Schneerson
1902–1994
The towering Jewish leader of the 20th century, known as "the Lubavitcher Rebbe," or simply as "the Rebbe." Born in southern Ukraine, the Rebbe escaped Nazi-occupied Europe, arriving in the U.S. in June 1941. The Rebbe inspired and guided the revival of traditional Judaism after the European devastation, impacting virtually every Jewish community the world over. The Rebbe often emphasized that the performance of just one additional good deed could usher in the era of Mashiach. The Rebbe's scholarly talks and writings have been printed in more than 200 volumes.

Forging a Relationship

The Clocktower

TEXT 7A

Devarim (Deuteronomy) 27:26

אָרוּר אֲשֶׁר לֹא יָקִים אֶת דִּבְרֵי הַתּוֹרָה הַזֹּאת לַעֲשׂוֹת אוֹתָם:

Cursed be he who does not uphold the words of this Torah, to fulfill them.

TEXT 7B

Jerusalem Talmud Tractate Sotah, 7:4

Jerusalem Talmud
A commentary to the Mishnah, compiled during the fourth and fifth centuries. The Jerusalem Talmud predates its Babylonian counterpart by 100 years and is written in both Hebrew and Aramaic. While the Babylonian Talmud is the most authoritative source for Jewish law, the Jerusalem Talmud remains an invaluable source for the spiritual, intellectual, ethical, historical, and legal traditions of Judaism.

אֲשֶׁר לֹא יָקִים וְכִי יֵשׁ תּוֹרָה נוֹפֶלֶת רַבִּי שִׁמְעוֹן בֶּן יָקִים אוֹמֵר זֶה הַחַזָּן.

"Cursed be he who does not uphold the words of this Torah," Rabbi Shimon ben Yakim says: This refers to the leader of the congregation.

TEXT 8

Nachmanides, Pirush Haramban to Devarim, loc cit.

> ולי נראה על החזן שאינו מקים ספר תורה על הצבור להראות פני
> כתיבתו לכל כמו שמפורש במסכת סופרים שמגביהין אותו ומראה
> פני כתיבתו לעם העומדים לימינו ולשמאלו ומחזירו לפניו ולאחריו
> שמצוה לכל אנשים והנשים לראות הכתוב ולכרוע ולומר וזאת
> התורה אשר שם משה וגו', וכן נוהגין.

I would suggest that this [statement of the Talmud] refers to a congregational leader who does not lift the Torah scroll for the congregation to show everyone the writing. As we find explicitly in tractate Sofrim, it is our custom to lift [the Torah] and display its writing to the congregation standing to his right, then his left, in front of him and in back of him, because it is a mitzvah for all men and women to see the writing and bow and say, "This is the Torah that Moses placed…"

Rabbi Moshe ben Nachman
(Nachmanides, Ramban)
1194–1270

Scholar, philosopher, author, and physician. Nachmanides was born in Spain and served as leader of Iberian Jewry. In 1263, he was summoned by King James of Aragon to a public disputation with Pablo Cristiani, a Jewish apostate. Though Nachmanides was the clear victor of the debate, he had to flee Spain because of the resulting persecution. He moved to Israel and helped reestablish communal life in Jerusalem. He authored a classic commentary on the Pentateuch and a commentary on the Talmud.

TEXT 9A

Rabbi Yitzchok Hutner, Pachad Yitzchok, p. 223

In bygone days, every city had a tall clock tower that was accessible by ladder only. It was said that the purpose of making the clock so high was twofold: First, so that it should be visible from a distance. But more importantly, because every person was expected to calibrate his or her watch according to its time, it was necessary to keep the clock out of reach. Otherwise, each person would tamper with it and adjust its time according to his or her watch, and the clock would become irrelevant.

TEXT 9B

Rabbi Yoel Malka, Kuntres Az Yashir, p. 2

Throughout the generations, we have been taught that Torah is exalted above all else; its place is in the heavens . . . and the Torah descended to earth to raise this world to heavenly heights.

[Unfortunately,] some mistakenly think that the Torah, now that it deals with earthly things, is subject to changes according to the winds of time and circumstance. But we know that the Torah stands on the

highest pedestal, and we must strive to attach ourselves to it. A person who merits this is a lofty individual.

This is the [symbolic] purpose of lifting the Torah scroll [in shul]: So that everyone should be made aware of Torah's exalted status. . . . And this is the reason why someone who does not raise the Torah is described as "cursed" . . . for he makes it seem as if it is no different from any other book.

The Clock Maker

TEXT 10

Talmud Tractate Shabbat, 105a

רבי יוחנן דידיה אמר "אנכי" נוטריקון אנא נפשי כתיבת יהבית.

Rabbi Yochanan taught, the word "Anochi," [the first word of the Ten Commandments, "I am the Lord your G-d, etc."] is an abbreviation for the statement, "I Myself wrote and gave" [the Torah].

TEXT 11A

Rabbi Shneur Zalman of Liadi, Tanya, ch. 4

Rabbi Shneur Zalman of Liadi
(Alter Rebbe)
1745–1812

Chasidic rebbe, halachic authority, and founder of the Chabad movement. The Alter Rebbe was born in Liozna, Belarus, and was among the principal students of the Magid of Mezeritch. His numerous works include the *Tanya*, an early classic containing the fundamentals of Chabad Chasidism, and *Shulchan Aruch HaRav*, an expanded and reworked code of Jewish law.

כמו שכתוב בזהר דאורייתא וקודשא בריך הוא כולא חד פירוש דאורייתא היא חכמתו ורצונו של הקדוש ברוך הוא והקדוש ברוך הוא בכבודו ובעצמו כולא חד כי הוא היודע והוא המדע וכו' כמו שכתוב לעיל בשם הרמב"ם . . .

[It is] explained in the Zohar, that the Torah and the Holy One, blessed be He, are one. The meaning of this is that the Torah, which is the wisdom and will of the Holy One, blessed be He, and His glorious Essence are one, because He is both the Knower and the Knowledge, and so on, as explained above in the name of Maimonides.

TEXT 11B

Ibid.

ואף דהקדוש ברוך הוא נקרא אין סוף ולגדולתו אין חקר ולית
מחשבה תפיסא ביה כלל וכן ברצונו וחכמתו כדכתיב אין חקר
לתבונתו וכתיב החקר אלוה תמצא וכתיב כי לא מחשבותי
מחשבותיכם. הנה על זה אמרו במקום שאתה מוצא גדולתו של
הקדוש ברוך הוא שם אתה מוצא ענותנותו וצמצם הקדוש ברוך
הוא רצונו וחכמתו בתרי"ג מצות התורה ובהלכותיהן ובצרופי
אותיות תנ"ך ודרשותיהן שבאגדות ומדרשי חכמינו ז"ל . . .
ולכן נמשלה התורה למים מה מים יורדים ממקום גבוה למקום
נמוך כך התורה ירדה ממקום כבודה שהיא רצונו וחכמתו יתברך
ואורייתא וקודשא בריך הוא כולא חד ולית מחשבה תפיסא
ביה כלל. ומשם נסעה וירדה בסתר המדרגות ממדרגה למדרגה
בהשתלשלות העולמות עד שנתלבשה בדברים גשמיים ועניני
עולם הזה שהן רוב מצות התורה ככולם והלכותיהן ובצרופי אותיות
גשמיות בדיו על הספר עשרים וארבעה ספרים שבתורה נביאים
וכתובים כדי שתהא כל מחשבה תפיסא בהן ואפילו בחינת דבור
ומעשה שלמטה ממדרגת מחשבה תפיסא בהן ומתלבשת בהן.

The Holy One, blessed be He, is called Ein Sof *("Infinite"), and "His greatness can never be fathomed," and "No thought can apprehend Him at all," and so are also His will and His wisdom, as it is written: "There is no searching of His understanding," and "Can you find G-d by searching?" and again: "For My thoughts are not your thoughts." Nevertheless . . . the Holy One, blessed be He, has compressed His will and wisdom within the 613 commandments of the Torah, and in their laws, as well as within the combination of the letters of the Torah, the Books of the Prophets and the Hagiographa (Writings), and in the exposition thereof, which are to be found in the Agadot and Midrashim of our rabbis of blessed memory…*

Therefore, the Torah has been compared to water, for just as water descends from a higher to a lower level, so has the Torah descended from its place of glory, which is His blessed will and wisdom; [for] the Torah and the Holy One, blessed be He, are one and the same and no thought can apprehend Him at all. Thence [the Torah] has progressively descended through hidden stages, stage after stage, with the descent of the worlds, until it clothed itself in corporeal substances and in things of this world, comprising almost all of the commandments of the Torah, their laws, and in the combinations of material letters, written with ink in a book, namely, the 24 volumes of the Torah, Prophets, and Hagiographa; all this in order that every thought should be able to apprehend them, and even the faculties of speech and action, which are on a lower level than thought, should be able to apprehend them and be clothed in them.

Recognizing Who, Not What

TEXT 12

Midrash Sifrei, Devarim 33:2

כשנגלה המקום ליתן תורה לישראל לא על ישראל בלבד הוא
נגלה, אלא על כל האומות: בתחילה הלך אצל בני עשו ואמר להם,
מקבלים אתם את התורה? אמרו לו, מה כתוב בה? אמר להם "לא
תרצח". אמרו, רבונו של עולם, כל עצמו של אותו אביהם רוצח
הוא, שנאמר "והידים ידי עשו", ועל כך הבטיחו אביו, שנאמר "על
חרבך תחיה".

הלך לו אצל בני עמון ומואב ואמר להם, מקבלים אתם את התורה?
אמרו לו מה כתוב בו? אמר להם "לא תנאף". אמרו לפניו, רבונו
של עולם, עצמה של ערוה להם היא, שנאמר "ותהרן שתי בנות
לוט מאביהם".

הלך ומצא בני ישמעאל, אמר להם, מקבלים אתם את התורה?
אמרו לו מה כתוב בה? אמר להם "לא תגנוב". אמרו לפניו, רבונו של
עולם, כל עצמו אביהם לסטים היה, שנאמר "והוא יהיה פרא אדם".
לא היתה אומה באומות שלא הלך ודבר, ודפק על פתחם מה ירצו
ויקבלו את התורה.

When G-d offered to give the Torah to Israel, He offered it not to Israel alone, but to all the nations.

First G-d went to the descendants of Esau and said to
them, "Will you accept the Torah?"

They responded, "What is written in it?"

G-d said to them, "You shall not murder."

They replied, "Master of the Universe, the very identity of our father [Esau] is a murderer, as it is said, '... But the hands are the hands of Esau,' and his father [Jacob] promised him the sword alone, 'By the sword you shall live.' We are not able to accept the Torah."

G-d went to the descendants of Ammon and Moab and said to them, "Will you accept the Torah?"

They said, "What is written in it?"

G-d replied, "You shall not commit adultery."

They said, "Master of the Universe, the very identity of our people comes from sexual immorality, as it is said, 'Thus were the two daughters of Lot pregnant from their father.' We are not able to accept the Torah."

G-d went to the descendants of Ishmael and said to them, "Will you accept the Torah?"

They said, "What is written in it?"

G-d answered, "You shall not steal."

They said, "Master of the Universe, the very identity of our father is stealing and robbery, as it is said, 'And Ishmael shall be a wild man, his hand against everyone and everyone's hand against him.' We are not able to accept the Torah."

There was no nation that G-d did not approach and ask if it wanted to accept the Torah.

Three Is the Magic Number

Great Is Peace

TEXT 13

Midrash Shemot Rabah, 12:3

Shemot Rabah

An early rabbinic commentary on the Book of Exodus. Midrash is the designation of a particular genre of rabbinic literature usually forming a running commentary on specific books of the Bible. *Shemot Rabah*, written mostly in Hebrew, provides textual exegeses, expounds upon the biblical narrative, and develops and illustrates moral principles. It was first printed in Constantinople in 1512 together with four other Midrashic works on the other four books of the Pentateuch.

גזר הקדוש ברוך הוא השמים שמים לה' והארץ נתן לבני אדם משל למה הדבר דומה למלך שגזר ואמר בני רומי לא ירדו לסוריא ובני סוריא לא יעלו לרומי.

כך כשברא הקדוש ברוך הוא את העולם גזר ואמר השמים שמים לה' והארץ נתן לבני אדם כשבקש ליתן התורה בטל גזירה ראשונה ואמר התחתונים יעלו לעליונים והעליונים ירדו לתחתונים ואני המתחיל שנאמר "וירד ה' על הר סיני" וכתיב "ואל משה אמר עלה אל ה'".

G-d decreed that the heavens are to be His realm, and only earth be given to man. To what is this analogous? To a king who decreed that the people of Rome cannot descend to Syria, and the people of Syria cannot ascend to Rome.

So, too, when G-d created the world, He decreed that the heavens be His realm and earth be the domain of man. When G-d wished to give the Torah, He rescinded this decree and stated, "The lower realms can now ascend to the higher, and the higher realms can descend to the lower—and I will be the first one." As it is stated, "And G-d descended upon the mountain, and it is stated further, "And G-d said to Moses to ascend to Him."

TEXT 14

Maimonides, Laws of Chanukah 4:14

Rabbi Moshe ben Maimon
(Maimonides, Rambam)
1135–1204
Halachist, philosopher, author, and physician. Maimonides was born in Córdoba, Spain. After the conquest of Córdoba by the Almohads, he fled Spain and eventually settled in Cairo, Egypt. There, he became the leader of the Jewish community and served as court physician to the vizier of Egypt. He is most noted for authoring the *Mishneh Torah*, an encyclopedic arrangement of Jewish law, and for his philosophical work, *Guide for the Perplexed.* His rulings on Jewish law are integral to the formation of halachic consensus.

גדול השלום שכל התורה ניתנה לעשות שלום בעולם שנאמר
"דרכיה דרכי נעם וכל נתיבותיה שלום".

Great is peace, for the Torah was given to establish peace on earth, as the verse states, "Its ways are pleasant, and all its paths are peace."

To This Day

TEXT 15

Rabbi Aharon Ibn Hayyim, Middot Aharon, Baraita of Rabbi Yishmael

עניין המדה הזאת הוא שהפסוקים המכחישין וסותרין זה את
זה הכחשה גמורה לא נוכל אנחנו להכריע ביניהם עד שהכתוב
השלישי יבא ויהיה הוא המכריע והראיה ממה שהוצרך הכתוב
להכריע בסתירה כזו ולא עזב את זה לדעת החכמים.

*The significance of this hermeneutical method is like
this: The two contradictory verses are a true contradiction, and not something that we can reconcile with our
own intellect; rather the third verse is necessary to do
the reconciliation. Proof positive of this is the very fact
that G-d did not leave the contradiction to the imagi-
nation of the sages and explicitly stated a third verse
to settle the matter.*

7

Naso

Strong as Samson

Watch What You Watch

PARSHAH OVERVIEW
Naso

Completing the head count of the Children of Israel taken in the Sinai Desert, a total of 8,580 Levite men between the ages of 30 and 50 are counted in a tally of those who will be doing the actual work of transporting the Tabernacle.

G-d communicates to Moses the law of the sotah, the wayward wife suspected of unfaithfulness to her husband. Also given is the law of the nazir, who forswears wine, lets his or her hair grow long, and is forbidden to become contaminated through contact with a dead body. Aaron and his descendants, the kohanim, are instructed on how to bless the people of Israel.

The leaders of the twelve tribes of Israel each bring their offerings for the inauguration of the altar. Although their gifts are identical, each is brought on a different day and is individually described by the Torah.

The Story of Shimshon

A Life of Valor

TEXT 1A

Shoftim (Judges) 14:5-6

וַיֵּרֶד שִׁמְשׁוֹן וְאָבִיו וְאִמּוֹ תִּמְנָתָה וַיָּבֹאוּ עַד כַּרְמֵי תִמְנָתָה וְהִנֵּה כְּפִיר אֲרָיוֹת שֹׁאֵג לִקְרָאתוֹ:
וַתִּצְלַח עָלָיו רוּחַ ה' וַיְשַׁסְּעֵהוּ כְּשַׁסַּע הַגְּדִי וּמְאוּמָה אֵין בְּיָדוֹ וְלֹא הִגִּיד לְאָבִיו וּלְאִמּוֹ אֵת אֲשֶׁר עָשָׂה:

And Samson and his father and mother went down to Timnath, and they came to the vineyards of Timnath, and behold, a young lion roared towards him.

Suddenly, a young lion roared at him. The spirit of G-d rushed on him, and he tore the lion apart bare-handed."

TEXT 1B

Ibid., 16:17

וַיַּגֶּד לָהּ אֶת כָּל לִבּוֹ וַיֹּאמֶר לָהּ מוֹרָה לֹא עָלָה עַל רֹאשִׁי כִּי נְזִיר אֱלֹהִים אֲנִי מִבֶּטֶן אִמִּי אִם גֻּלַּחְתִּי וְסָר מִמֶּנִּי כֹחִי וְחָלִיתִי וְהָיִיתִי כְּכָל הָאָדָם:

And he told her all his heart, and said to her, "A razor has not come upon my head, for I am a Nazirite to G-d from my mother's womb. If I will be shaven, then my strength will leave me, and I shall become weak and be like any man."

A Holy Warrior

TEXT 2

Talmud Tractate Sotah, 10a

ואמר רבי יוחנן שמשון דן את ישראל כאביהם שבשמים שנאמר "דן ידין עמו כאחד וגו'". ואמר רבי יוחנן שמשון על שמו של הקדוש ברוך הוא נקרא שנאמר "כי שמש ומגן ה' אלהים וגו'". אלא מעתה לא ימחה? אלא מעין שמו של הקדוש ברוך הוא מה הקדוש ברוך הוא מגין על כל העולם כולו אף שמשון מגין בדורו על ישראל.

Babylonian Talmud

A literary work of monumental proportions that draws upon the legal, spiritual, intellectual, ethical, and historical traditions of Judaism. The 37 tractates of the Babylonian Talmud contain the teachings of the Jewish sages from the period after the destruction of the Second Temple through the fifth century CE. It has served as the primary vehicle for the transmission of the Oral Law and the education of Jews over the centuries; it is the entry point for all subsequent legal, ethical, and theological Jewish scholarship.

Rabbi Yochanan said: Samson judged the Jewish people just as G-d does, as the verse states, "Dan will judge his nation, as one." That is, the judge from the tribe of Dan, Shimshon, judges like G-d judges.

Rabbi Yochanan said: Samson is called by the name of G-d, as the verse states, "A sun and a shield is the Lord G-d." The word "shemesh," sun, has the same root at the name Shimshon.

But now, if Shimshon's name was really the name of G-d, then we would not be permitted to erase it. Rather, it is merely like *the name of G-d: Just as G-d protects the entire world, so did Shimshon guard the Jewish people in his generation.*

A Match Made in Heaven

TEXT 3

Shoftim (Judges) 14:3-4

וַיֹּאמֶר לוֹ אָבִיו וְאִמּוֹ הַאֵין בִּבְנוֹת אַחֶיךָ וּבְכָל עַמִּי אִשָּׁה כִּי אַתָּה הוֹלֵךְ לָקַחַת אִשָּׁה מִפְּלִשְׁתִּים הָעֲרֵלִים וַיֹּאמֶר שִׁמְשׁוֹן אֶל אָבִיו אוֹתָהּ קַח לִי כִּי הִיא יָשְׁרָה בְעֵינָי:

וְאָבִיו וְאִמּוֹ לֹא יָדְעוּ כִּי מֵה' הִיא כִּי תֹאֲנָה הוּא מְבַקֵּשׁ מִפְּלִשְׁתִּים וּבָעֵת הַהִיא פְּלִשְׁתִּים מֹשְׁלִים בְּיִשְׂרָאֵל:

Samson's father and mother said to him, "Is there no one among the daughters of your own kin and among all our people that you wish to marry? Must you go take a wife from the uncircumcised Philistines?"

Now his father and mother did not know that it was from G-d, that he sought a pretense against the Philistines; now, at that time, the Philistines were ruling over Israel.

Room in the Law

TEXT 4A

Rabbi David Kimchi, Radak, to Shoftim 13:4

ויש לתמוה היאך מי שצוה עליו הבורא יתברך להיות קדושתו מן
הבטן איך נטמא בבנות הפלשתים?

והנראה בזה כי הנשים אשר לקח בתמנה ובעזה ובנחל שורק גייר
אותן והשיבן לדת ישראל כי חלילה כי משופט ישראל ומושיעם
להתחתן בפלשתים ועובר על לאו דלא תתחתן בם אשר חמור
מאד ומביא את האדם לידי כפירה בבורא יתברך ויתעלה כמו
שאמר כי יסיר את בנך מאחרי. ולא נמצא בכתוב שנענש על זה
ולא נאמר עליו שעשה רע בעיני ה׳ והיה הבורא יתעלה מצליחו
בכל אשר יפנה, וכן אמר הכתוב "כי מה׳ היא", כלומר לקחתו אשה
מבנות פלשתים מה׳ היתה.

ורצון האל ית׳ היה בזה כי בודאי היה מגייר אותן ומשיבן אל דת
ישראל, ואף על פי כן סבה היתה מאת השם לקחת אשה מפלשתים
להנקם בהם כי נראה כי ישראל שבאותו הדור לא היו יראים השם
כל כך שיושיעם תשועה שלימה מיד פלשתים כי כל ימי שמשון
היו מושלים פלשתים בישראל כי מה שאמר הכתוב ויתנם ה׳ ביד
פלשתים ארבעים שנה עשרים של שמשון בכללם על כרחך לפי
חשבון השנים ולא היו ישראל נלחמים בהם כי אם שמשון לבדו
ולפיכך לא היה לפלשתים טענה להלחם בישראל מפני שמשון
כי לא היה ברשותם והוא לבדו היה עושה הרעות בפלשתים ועם
פלשתים היה שוכן בעוד שהיה מריע להם ומיראתם אותו גם כן
היו נמנעים מלהלחם בישראל לפיכך כשבקשוהו פלשתים מבני
יהודה כשהלך לסלע עיטם מסרוהו להם וכן עדת דבורים בגוית
האריה ודבש וכן היות אשת שמשון למרעהו הכל סבה להנקם
מפלשתים יתברך האל אשר לו נתכנו עלילות וסבות ומאתו הכל.

Rabbi David Kimchi
(Radak)
1160–1235
Provençal medieval
grammarian and biblical
exegete. Rabbi Kimchi wrote
a comprehensive exposition
of Hebrew grammar
called *Miklol*, and *Sefer
Hashorashim*, a dictionary
of the Bible. He is probably
best known for his classic
commentaries on the Bible.

*It is extremely troubling, how can an individual sancti-
fied at G-d's command from the womb involve himself
with the impure daughters of the Philistines?*

*Rather, the women taken in Timnah and Gaza and
Nachal Shurak were all converted when Shimshon
brought them to the Jewish faith. G-d forbid to think
that a judge and savior of Israel married Philistines in
direct violation of the Torah's command. All the more
so when this prohibition is particularly severe and
brings one to heresy against G-d, as the verse states,
"For they will turn your children away from me." We
never find in the story of Samson that he is punished
for these marriages, or that he did evil in the eyes of
G-d. On the contrary, G-d brought him success in all of
his endeavors. This is why the verse says the marriage
was divinely inspired—G-d wanted him to marry the
Philistine woman, whom he certainly converted.*

*If they converted, then why was it important that
they come from the Philistines? Because G-d wanted
Samson to avenge the oppression of Israel upon
their oppressors. The generation of Samson was not
deserving of full and direct redemption from their
enemies, and in Samson's times the Philistines ruled
over Israel. Israel did not war against them. Samson
warred against them alone and was perceived as a
"rogue agent," rather than as a warrior for whom the
Jews were responsible. Marrying Philistine wives was
a pretext for dwelling near them and attacking them,*

without any responsibility devolving upon the other Jews, and the entire plan came from G-d.

TEXT 4B

Maimonides, Mishneh Torah, Laws of Forbidden Relations, 13:14-16

רבינו הזקן קבל מרבי מרדכי הצדיק ששמע מהבעל שם טוב: עס
קומט אראפ א נשמה אויף דער וועלט און לעבט אפ זיבעציג אכציג
יאהר, צוליב טאן א אידען א טובה בגשמיות ובפרט אין רוחניות.

אל יעלה על דעתך ששמשון המושיע את ישראל או שלמה מלך
ישראל שנקרא ידיד ה' נשאו נשים נכריות בגיותן... ולפי שגייר שלמה
נשים ונשאן וכן שמשון גייר ונשא.

Do not imagine that Samson, the savior of Israel, or Solomon, king of Israel and friend of G-d, married non-Jewish women in a full Gentile state. . . . Rather, Solomon converted his wives and married them. Samson, too, converted his wife and married her.

Rabbi Moshe ben Maimon (Maimonides, Rambam) 1135–1204
Halachist, philosopher, author, and physician. Maimonides was born in Córdoba, Spain. After the conquest of Córdoba by the Almohads, he fled Spain and eventually settled in Cairo, Egypt. There, he became the leader of the Jewish community and served as court physician to the vizier of Egypt. He is most noted for authoring the *Mishneh Torah*, an encyclopedic arrangement of Jewish law, and for his philosophical work, *Guide for the Perplexed*. His rulings on Jewish law are integral to the formation of halachic consensus.

Lesson 7 / Strong as Samson

The Power of Vision

Attendants of Transgression

TEXT 5

Jerusalem Talmud Tractate Berachot, 9a

Jerusalem Talmud
A commentary to the Mishnah, compiled during the fourth and fifth centuries. The Jerusalem Talmud predates its Babylonian counterpart by 100 years and is written in both Hebrew and Aramaic. While the Babylonian Talmud is the most authoritative source for Jewish law, the Jerusalem Talmud remains an invaluable source for the spiritual, intellectual, ethical, historical, and legal traditions of Judaism.

אמר רבי לוי ליבא ועינא תרין סרסורין דחטאה דכתיב "תנה בני לבך לי ועיניך דרכי תצרנה". אמר הקדוש ברוך הוא אי יהבת לי לבך ועיניך אנא ידע דאת לי.

Rabbi Levi said: The heart and the eyes are the two agents that bring one to sin, as the verse states, "My son, give me your heart and let your eyes observe my ways." G-d says, "If you give me your heart and your eyes, I will know that you are mine."

TEXT 6

Bamidbar (Numbers) 15:39

וְהָיָה לָכֶם לְצִיצִת וּרְאִיתֶם אֹתוֹ וּזְכַרְתֶּם אֶת כָּל מִצְוֺת ה' וַעֲשִׂיתֶם אֹתָם וְלֹא תָתוּרוּ אַחֲרֵי לְבַבְכֶם וְאַחֲרֵי עֵינֵיכֶם אֲשֶׁר אַתֶּם זֹנִים אַחֲרֵיהֶם:

This shall be fringes for you, and when you see it, you will remember all the commandments of the Lord to perform them, and you shall not wander after your hearts and after your eyes after which you are going astray. (The eye sees, and the heart desires. —Rashi)

The Greatest Pleasure

TEXT 7

Rabbi Shneur Zalman of Liadi,
Maamarei Admur Hazaken, 5569, p. 126

Rabbi Shneur Zalman of Liadi (Alter Rebbe)
1745–1812
Chasidic rebbe, halachic authority, and founder of the Chabad movement. The Alter Rebbe was born in Liozna, Belarus, and was among the principal students of the Magid of Mezeritch. His numerous works include the *Tanya*, an early classic containing the fundamentals of Chabad Chasidism, and *Shulchan Aruch HaRav*, an expanded and reworked code of Jewish law.

אנו רואים שיש התלבשות כח התענוג בחוש הראיה יותר משאר החושים כי גם שיש הארת העונג בכל החושים כמו בחוש הריח שמריח דבר בושם טוב שיערב לנפש מאז, וכן חוש השמיעה כששומע קול ערב שמתענג מאד בנפשו הנה כל זה אין לו ערך לגבי כח התענוג שמתענג בנפשו מהסתכלות העין בדבר ציור נאה, כמו דירה נאה מאד או בגדי תפארת למראה או אבנים טובות מבהיקים ביופי, וכל דבר נחמד למראה ביותר. שהרי אמרו רז"ל העין רואה והלב חומד הרי שהקדים העין רואה ללב חומד כי... העין הרואה בדבר הנחמד, שם מלובש כח התענוג ביותר עד שמחמתו נתפעל החימוד בלב.

וזהו שכתוב "ולא תתורו כו'" לפי שיש בו בחינת כח חזק מן הארת התענוג עד שימשיך את הלב לחימוד.

We find that the soul's faculty of pleasure and satisfaction is invested more in the sense of sight than any of the other senses. There is actually limited expression of pleasure in every sense, such as the olfactory, when one smells a pleasant perfume, and it pleases the soul, or the auditory, when one hears a sweet voice, and it creates a profound feeling of satisfaction in one's soul. None of these pleasures, however, compare to the satisfaction of perceiving pleasant forms with one's eyes, such as pleasing architecture, beautiful clothing, or the glittering splendor of fine gem stones. All things are most coveted when they are perceived by the eyes, as the sages say, "The eye sees and the heart desires." "Eyes seeing" precedes the words "heart's desire" for good reason ... inasmuch as the soul's capacity of pleasure is vested in the eye that beholds a desirable thing, rousing the heart to lustful passion.

This is why the verse says, "Do not stray after your heart and after your eyes." The eyes bring so much pleasure to a person that they can arouse the heart to powerful desire.

TEXT 8

Rabi Shalom Dovber of Lubavitch, Kuntres Haavodah, ch. 2

אשר באמת הראיה, וכל שכן ההסתכלות היא הסבה הגורמת לכל
דבר רע והיא המביאה לרע גמור ר"ל, וכמאמר עינא ולבא תרין
סרסורין דעבירה העין רואה והלב חומד וכל המסתכל כו' סוף בא
לידי עבירה, וכנודע דעיקר התענוג הוא בחוש הראיה . . . ועל כן
הראיה מעורר התענוג שבנפש . . .

ועל כן יתגבר כארי להגדיר את עצמו בכל תוקף ועוז וגם אם יהיה
ניכר אל יחוש לשיחות כני אדם. והלא בדבר הנוגע לחיי הנפש
בגשמיות אינם מביטים על שום דבר, וכל שכן בהנוג על חיי הנפש
הרוחני, וההכבדות בזה היא רק בעת הראשונה שצריך להכביד על
עצמו ולהתגבר על טבעו ורצונו ובמשך הזמן יתרגל כך. ובהגדרה
זאת ימצא מנוחה לנפשו מכמה רעות ובלבולים ואז יוכל לעבוד
עבודתו. וביגיעתו יפעול ישועות בנפשו בעזרתו יתברך.

Rabbi Shalom Dovber Schneersohn
(Rashab)
1860–1920

Chasidic rebbe. Rabbi Shalom Dovber became the fifth leader of the Chabad movement upon the passing of his father, Rabbi Shmuel of Lubavitch. He established the Lubavitch network of *yeshivot* called Tomchei Temimim. He authored many volumes of Chasidic discourses and is renowned for his lucid and thorough explanations of kabbalistic concepts.

Sight, and certainly full-on visual examination, is the cause of all negative matters in divine service. It is a relatively small act that brings one to an act of pure evil, G-d forbid. As it is said, "The eye and the heart are the two agents of sin—the eye sees and the heart desires." Whoever looks eventually comes to sin; as is known, the eyes are the main seat of pleasure. . . . It is indeed sight that arouses the soul's pleasure…

Therefore, one must strengthen him-or herself like a lion, and use all [his or her] power to limit what [he or she sees.] Even if others realize how carefully you guard your eyes, you must not be moved by any mockery. After all, if you must do something embar-rassing to save your physical life, you don't care what anyone says. All the more so, one's spiritual life should not be risked for what others think. The hardest part of controlling one's eyes is the first time, when one's nature must be conquered. Eventually, guarding the eyes becomes habit. Practicing guarding the eyes will secure inner peace from several evils and confounding forces, and will enable the person to serve G-d. With hard work, he will be able to save his soul from the depths, with G-d's help.

Shimshon's Downfall

TEXT 9

Talmud Tractate Sotah, 9b

תנו רבנן שמשון בעיניו מרד שנאמר "ויאמר שמשון אל אביו אותה
קח לי כי היא ישרה בעיני", לפיכך נקרו פלשתים את עיניו שנאמר
"ויאחזוהו פלשתים וינקרו את עיניו".
איני? –והכתיב "ואביו ואמו לא ידעו כי מה' היא"!
כי אזל, מיהא, בתר ישרותיה אזל.

Our sages taught: Samson rebelled with his eyes, as the verse states, "And Samson said to his father, 'Take her for me, for she is upright in my eyes.'" Therefore, he was punished, measure for measure, and the Philistines gouged out his eyes, as it is stated, "The Philistines took hold of him and gouged out his eyes."

Was he really punished for the involvement of his eyes? Did the verse not state, "His father and his mother did not know that the marriage was divinely inspired?"

When he approached her, he approached her based on his personal attraction.

An Eye for an Eye

Shimshon's Vengeance

TEXT 10

Shoftim (Judges) 16:28

וַיִּקְרָא שִׁמְשׁוֹן אֶל ה' וַיֹּאמַר אֲדֹ-נָי ה' זָכְרֵנִי נָא וְחַזְּקֵנִי נָא אַךְ הַפַּעַם
הַזֶּה הָאֱלֹקִים וְאִנָּקְמָה נְקַם אַחַת מִשְּׁתֵי עֵינַי מִפְּלִשְׁתִּים:

Samson called out to G-d and said, "G-d, Lord, please remember me, please strengthen me, so that I can, this one time, have one act of vengeance for my two eyes against the Philistines."

TEXT 11

Rabbi David Altschuler, Metzudat David to Shoftim 16:28

Rabbi David Altschuler
1687–1769

Biblical commentator. Rabbi Altschuler, a renowned Polish rabbi, wrote two biblical commentaries that are considered crucial to Bible study: the *Metzudat David* expounds upon the meaning of the text, and *Metzudat Tsion* provides definitions. After he died a martyr's death, his works were published by his son, Rabbi Hillel Altschuler, under the name *Metzudot*.

רבינו הזקן קבל מרבי מרדכי הצדיק ששמע מהבעל שם טוב: עס
קומט אראפ א נשמה אויף דער וועלט און לעבט אף זיבעציג אכציג
יאהר, צוליב טאן א אידען א טובה בגשמיות ובפרט אין רוחניות.

"נקם אחת". עוד פעם אחת אנקום מפלשתים על מה שנקרו שתי
עיני ורבותינו זכרונם לברכה אמרו שאמר, מה שנקרו עין אחת אנקום,
והשנית תהיה שמורה לעולם הבא.

"One Revenge/Revenge One." The straightforward reading is, "Please give me one more revenge against the Philistines for putting out my eyes." The sages add in the Midrash that Samson was saying, "Please let me avenge one eye that was taken from me, and let the other wait for me in the World to Come."

A Spark in the Right Eye

TEXT 12

Rabbi Yosef Chaim of Baghdad, Ben Yehoyada to Sotah 10a

הא דבקש על עין אחת דוקא, עיין פירוש רש"י ז"ל. ועוד נראה לי בס"ד, כבאדם יש ב' עינים אחת ימנית ואחת שמאלית, וכנגד זה יש לו שני ראיות במעשיו, את הימנית דהיינו שמכוין לשם שמים, ואחת שמאלית שמכוון להנאתו. אך יש אדם שכל ראיה שלו היא לשם שמים דוקא, דהיינו ימנית, ויש הכל שמאלית שמכוון להנאתו דוקא, ויש משתמש בשניהם שהוא רואה לכאן ולכאן.

והנה שמשון בענין התחברותו עם נשים נכריות מפלשתים לא הלך אחר עין השמאלית, אלא היה לו ראיה ימנית גם כן, שכיון לשם שמים כאשר כתבנו לעיל, כדי לברר נ"ק מן הקליפה שלהם. ולכן כאשר ניקרו פלשתים את עיניו בשביל זה העון שהיה בידו, לא היה מן הדין לנקר אלא רק עין השמאלית, כדי לכפר על ראיה השמאלית שהיה מתכוון להנאתו גם כן, אך הם הוסיפו ברע שניקרו את שתיהם, על דרך מה שאמר הכתוב "אני קצפתי מעט והמה עזרו לרעה", לכך בקש לנקום מהם על אחת דוקא, שלקתה שלא כדין על חמס בכפו.

Rabbi Yosef Chaim of Baghdad (*Ben Ish Chai*) 1834–1909 Sefardic halachist and kabbalist. Rabbi Yosef Chaim succeeded his father as chief rabbi of Baghdad in 1859, and is best known as author of his halachic work, *Ben Ish Chai*, by which title he is also known. Also popular is his commentary on the homiletical sections of the Talmud, called *Ben Yehoyada*.

Samson requested vengeance for one eye specifically. See Rashi on this matter. Another explanation that seems appropriate to me: A human being has two eyes, a right eye and a left eye, and accordingly, he has two ways of looking at his actions: His "right-side vision" sees actions that are for the sake of heaven, and his "left-side vision" sees only matters to his own benefit. There are some people who see only actions for the sake of heaven, with their "right," and there are others who see only with their "left," for their own benefit. There are also those who use both sides and see both perspectives.

Shimshon, with regard to marrying his Philistine wives, didn't follow the left eye alone, but also the right eye—his intentions were for the sake of heaven, to refine the holy sparks from the spiritual concealment of the Philistines. Therefore, when they put out both of his eyes as punishment for his transgression, they really only should have put out his left—the one that transgressed. Instead, they added to the punishment he deserved. This is why Shimshon demanded revenge for just one eye, which was taken from him unjustly.

Two Good Eyes

TEXT 13

Rabbi Yosef Yitzchak Schneersohn of Lubavitch,
Sefer HaSichot 5691 p. 1584

ווען איך בין אַלט געווען פיר יאָר האָב איך גיפרעגט בּא דעם טאַטן
פאַר וואָס האָט דער אויבּערשטער ברוך הוא בּעשאַפּן אַ מענטשן
צווייי אויגן און איין מויל, און איין נאָז. האָט ער מיך גיפרעגט צו
ווייס איך אלף בית, ועניתי הן. פרעגט מיך ווידער דער טאַטע, צי
ווייסטו אז עס איז פאַראַן אַ שין און אַ סין, און וואָס איז דער חילוק
פון זיי. ועניתי לו, אז אַ שין איז די פּינטעלע פון דער רעכטער זייט
און סין איז די פּינטעלע פון דער לינקער זייט.
האָט מיר דער טאַטע געזאָגט, פאַראַן זאַכן וואָס מיא דאַרף אויף
זיי קוקן מיט דער רעכטער אויג, און פאַראַן זאַכן וואָס מיא דאַרף
אויף זיי קוקן מיט דער לינקער אויג. אין אַ סידור און אויף אַ אידן
דאַרפמען קוקן מיט דער רעכטער אויג, און אויף אַ צוקערקע און
אַ צאַצקע מיט דער לינקער אויג. און פון יעמולט אָן האָט זער
איינגעוואָרצלט די זאַך אז אויף אַ אידן וועל ער זאָל ניט זיין און וי
ער זאָל ניט זיין דאַרף מען קוקן בּעין יפה.

Rabbi Yosef Yitzchak Schneersohn
(Rayatz, Frierdiker Rebbe, Previous Rebbe)
1880–1950

Chasidic rebbe, prolific writer, and Jewish activist. Rabbi Yosef Yitzchak, the sixth leader of the Chabad movement, actively promoted Jewish religious practice in Soviet Russia and was arrested for these activities. After his release from prison and exile, he settled in Warsaw, Poland, from where he fled Nazi occupation, and arrived in New York in 1940. Settling in Brooklyn, Rabbi Schneersohn worked to revitalize American Jewish life. His son-in law, Rabbi Menachem Mendel Schneerson, succeeded him as the leader of the Chabad movement.

When I was four years old, I asked my father why the Holy One, blessed be He, created man with two eyes and one mouth and nose. He asked me whether I knew the Hebrew alphabet, and I told him yes. My father asked me further whether I knew about the letters "shin" and "sin" and the difference between them. I told him that a "shin" has the dot on the right side and the "sin" has the dot on the left side.

My father told me, "There are some things a person must look at with the right eye, and others he must look at with the left eye. On a siddur or a fellow Jew, one must look with the right eye, whereas on a candy or toy, he should use the left eye." From that day on, I have never forgotten that a fellow Jew, no matter who they are nor what their quality, must be looked upon favorably.

Learning from What We See

TEXT 14

The Lubavitcher Rebbe, Hayom Yom, Entry for 9 Iyar

Rabbi Menachem Mendel Schneerson
1902–1994

The towering Jewish leader of the 20th century, known as "the Lubavitcher Rebbe," or simply as "the Rebbe." Born in southern Ukraine, the Rebbe escaped Nazi-occupied Europe, arriving in the U.S. in June 1941. The Rebbe inspired and guided the revival of traditional Judaism after the European devastation, impacting virtually every Jewish community the world over. The Rebbe often emphasized that the performance of just one additional good deed could usher in the era of Mashiach. The Rebbe's scholarly talks and writings have been printed in more than 200 volumes.

מורנו הבעל שם טוב אמר: כל דבר ודבר אשר האדם רואה או שומע, הוא הוראת הנהגה בעבודת השם. וזהו ענין העבודה, להבין ולהשכיל מכל דרך בעבודת השם.

Our teacher the Baal Shem Tov said: Every single thing one sees or hears is an instruction for his conduct in the service of G-d. This is the idea of avodah, *service, to comprehend and discern in all things a way in which to serve G-d. [Chabad.org translation]*

TEXT 15

Talmud Tractate Sotah, 2a

דתניא רבי אומר למה נסמכה פרשת נזיר לפרשת סוטה לומר לך
שכל הרואה סוטה בקלקולה יזיר עצמו מן היין.

We are taught: Rebbi said, "Why is the portion of the Nazir adjacent to the portion of the Sotah in the Torah? To teach us that whoever witnessed the Sotah in her disgrace should renounce wine."

TEXT 16

Rabbi Tzadok Hakohen of Lublin Pri Tzadik, Naso 13:1

ולכן נזכר בתורה שבכתב סוטה קודם נזיר שמזה שנזדמן לראות
זאת צריך להבין שבטח צריך להזיר עצמו מן היין. ובתורה שבעל
פה בגמרא נסדר נזיר קודם סוטה. והוא כענין שאמרם ז"ל באבות
"איזהו דרך טוב וכו' הרואה את הנולד", היינו מצד חכמתו רואה
מקודם שמזדמן לפניו מה שיוכל להולד מזה ומזיר עצמו מן היין
וכן בכל ענינים.

The story of the Sotah precedes the laws of the Nazir in Scripture, because the person who witnesses the Sotah understands that witnessing such a spectacle should compel him to renounce wine. In the Oral Torah, however, Nazir precedes Sotah. The idea behind that is in the spirit of what our sages say in Tractate Avot, "What is the correct path ... the one who sees the future." That is, in their wisdom, they can already see from what is before them what will happen in the future. Thus, they renounce wine preemptively.

BEHAALOTECHA

Desiring Desire

Is It Okay to Tempt Yourself?

PARSHAH OVERVIEW
Behaalotecha

Aaron is commanded to raise light in the lamps of the menorah, and the tribe of Levi is initiated into the service in the Sanctuary.

A "Second Passover" is instituted in response to the petition "Why should we be deprived?" by a group of Jews who were unable to bring the Passover offering in its appointed time because they were ritually impure. G-d instructs Moses on the procedures for Israel's journeys and encampments in the desert, and the people journey in formation from Mount Sinai, where they had been camped for nearly a year.

The people are dissatisfied with their "bread from heaven" (the manna), and demand that Moses supply them with meat. Moses appoints 70 elders, to whom he imparts his spirit, to assist him in the burden of governing the people. Miriam speaks negatively of Moses and is punished with leprosy; Moses prays for her healing, and the entire community waits seven days for her recovery.

Temptation and the Human Condition

Hungry Jews

TEXT 1

Bamidbar (Numbers) 11:4-6

וְהָאסַפְסֻף אֲשֶׁר בְּקִרְבּוֹ הִתְאַוּוּ תַּאֲוָה וַיָּשֻׁבוּ וַיִּבְכּוּ גַּם בְּנֵי יִשְׂרָאֵל
וַיֹּאמְרוּ מִי יַאֲכִלֵנוּ בָּשָׂר:
זָכַרְנוּ אֶת הַדָּגָה אֲשֶׁר נֹאכַל בְּמִצְרַיִם חִנָּם אֵת הַקִּשֻּׁאִים וְאֵת
הָאֲבַטִּחִים וְאֶת הֶחָצִיר וְאֶת הַבְּצָלִים וְאֶת הַשּׁוּמִים:
וְעַתָּה נַפְשֵׁנוּ יְבֵשָׁה אֵין כֹּל בִּלְתִּי אֶל הַמָּן עֵינֵינוּ:

But the multitude among them began to have strong cravings. Then even the Children of Israel once again began to cry, and they said, "Who will feed us meat?

"We remember the fish that we ate in Egypt free of charge, the cucumbers, the watermelons, the leeks, the onions, and the garlic.

"But now, our bodies are dried out, for there is nothing at all; we have nothing but manna to look at."

Fleeing Flocks?

TEXT 2

Shemot (Exodus) 12:38

וַיִּסְעוּ בְנֵי יִשְׂרָאֵל מֵרַעְמְסֵס סֻכֹּתָה כְּשֵׁשׁ מֵאוֹת אֶלֶף רַגְלִי הַגְּבָרִים
לְבַד מִטָּף:
וְגַם עֵרֶב רַב עָלָה אִתָּם וְצֹאן וּבָקָר מִקְנֶה כָּבֵד מְאֹד:

The Children of Israel journeyed from Rameses to Succoth, about six hundred thousand on foot, the men, besides the young children.

And also, a great mixed multitude went up with them, and flocks and cattle, very much livestock.

Looking to Complain

Rabbi Shlomo Yitzchaki (Rashi)
1040–1105

Most noted biblical and Talmudic commentator. Born in Troyes, France, Rashi studied in the famed *yeshivot* of Mainz and Worms. His commentaries on the Pentateuch and the Talmud, which focus on the straightforward meaning of the text, appear in virtually every edition of the Talmud and Bible.

TEXT 3

Rashi on Bamidbar 11:4

"מי יאכלנו בשר." וכי לא היה להם בשר, והלא כבר נאמר (שמות יב, לח) וגם ערב רב עלה אתם וצאן ובקר וגו'. ואם תאמר אכלום, והלא בכניסתם לארץ נאמר (במדבר לב, א) ומקנה רב היה לבני ראובן וגו', אלא שמבקשים עלילה.

"Who will feed us meat?" Did they not have meat? Does it not say, "Also a great mixed multitude went up with them, and flocks and cattle?" You might argue that they had already eaten them. But when they were about to enter the Land, is it not written that, "The children of Reuben had much cattle?"

Unfounded Claims

TEXT 4A

Maimonides, Shemonah Perakim, ch.6

Rabbi Moshe ben Maimon
(Maimonides, Rambam)
1135–1204

Halachist, philosopher, author, and physician. Maimonides was born in Córdoba, Spain. After the conquest of Córdoba by the Almohads, he fled Spain and eventually settled in Cairo, Egypt. There, he became the leader of the Jewish community and served as court physician to the vizier of Egypt. He is most noted for authoring the *Mishneh Torah*, an encyclopedic arrangement of Jewish law, and for his philosophical work, *Guide for the Perplexed*. His rulings on Jewish law are integral to the formation of halachic consensus.

אמרו הפילוסופים שהמושל בנפשו אף על פי שעשה המעשים
הטובים והחשובים, הוא עושה אותם והוא מתאוה אל הפעולות
הרעות ונכסף אליהם, ויכבוש את יצרו, ויחלוק בפעולותיו על מה
שיעירוהו אליו כחותיו ותאוותו ותכונת נפשו, ויעשה הטובות והוא
מצטער בעשיתם (ונזוק), אבל החסיד הוא נמשך בפעולתו אחר
מה שתעירהו אליו תאותו ותכונתו ויעשה הטובות והוא מתאוה
ונכסף אליהן, ובהסכמה מן הפילוסופים שהחסיד יותר חשוב ויותר
שלם מן המושל בנפשו, אבל אמרו שאפשר שיהיה המושל בנפשו
כחסיד בענינים רבים, ומעלתו למטה ממנו בהכרח, להיותו מתאוה
לפועל הרע, ואע"פ שאינו עושה אותו מפני שתשוקתו לרע היא
תכונה רעה בנפש.

Philosophers have noted that a person who overcomes his inclinations may act favorably and respectably, but deep down still desires evil. He defies his natural feelings, which is for him a painful process. Conversely, a pious person is naturally drawn to good.

The consensus among philosophers is that the naturally pious individual is more respectable and healthier than he who must overcome his inclinations. This latter individual may be pious in certain ways but is inferior to the naturally pious individual by dint of the fact that he has that desire for evil in him, even if he doesn't act upon it.

TEXT 4B

Talmud Tractate Sukkah, 52a

Babylonian Talmud

A literary work of monumental proportions that draws upon the legal, spiritual, intellectual, ethical, and historical traditions of Judaism. The 37 tractates of the Babylonian Talmud contain the teachings of the Jewish sages from the period after the destruction of the Second Temple through the fifth century CE. It has served as the primary vehicle for the transmission of the Oral Law and the education of Jews over the centuries; it is the entry point for all subsequent legal, ethical, and theological Jewish scholarship.

כי הא דאביי שמעיה לההוא גברא דקאמר לההיא אתתא נקדים
וניזיל באורחא אמר איזיל אפרשינהו מאיסורא אזל בתרייהו תלתא
פרסי באגמא כי הוו פרשי מהדדי שמעינהו דקא אמרי אורחין
רחיקא וצוותין בסימא אמר אביי אי אי מאן דסני לי הוה לא הוה מצי
לאוקומיה נפשיה אזל תלא נפשיה בעיבורא דדשא ומצטער אתא
ההוא סבא תנא ליה כל הגדול מחבירו יצרו גדול הימנו.

Abaye once heard a certain man say to a certain woman: Let us rise early and go on the road. [Upon hearing this,] Abaye said to himself: I will go and accompany them and prevent them from violating the prohibition [that they certainly intend to violate.]

He went after them for a distance of three parasangs in a marsh among the reeds [and they did not engage in any wrongful activity]. When they were taking leave of each other, he heard that they were saying: We traveled a long distance together, and the company was pleasant company.

Abaye said: If, instead of that man, it had been one whom I hate, [a euphemism for himself], he would not have been able to restrain himself from sinning. After becoming aware of so great a shortcoming, he went and leaned against the doorpost, feeling regret.

A certain elder came and taught him: The greater the person, the greater the inclination.

TEXT 4C

Maimonides, Shemonah Perakim, Ibid.

וכאשר חקרנו דברי חכמים בזה הענין, נמצא להם שהמתאוה
לעבירות והנכסף אליהם יותר חשוב ויותר שלם מאשר לא מתאוה
אליהם, ולא יצטער בהנחתם, עד שאמרו שכל אשר יהיה האיש
יותר חשוב ויותר שלם תהיה תשוקתו לעבירות והצטערו בהנחתן
יותר גדול, והביאו בזה הדברים ואמרו כל הגדול מחבירו יצרו גדול
ממנו, ולא דים זה אלא שאמרו ששכר המושל בנפשו גדול לפי רוב
צערו במשלו בנפשו, ואמרו לפום צערא אגרא, ויותר מזה שהם
ציוו שיהא האדם מתאוה לעבירות, והזהירו מלומר שאני בטבעי
לא אתאוה לזאת העבירה ואע"פ שלא תאסרה התורה, והוא אמרם
רבן שמעון בן גמליאל אומר לא יאמר אדם אי אפשי לאכול בשר
בחלב, אי אפשי ללבוש שעטנז, אי אפשי לבוא על הערוה, אלא
אפשי ומה אעשה ואבי שבשמים גזר עלי.

Upon comprehensive research of the sages' works on this topic, we will find that a person who is inclined to sin and desires sin is greater and more complete than he who does not have such desires and who feels no pain in abstaining from sin. Indeed, the sages have said that the greater and more whole a person is, the greater his passion for sin and the greater the difficulty in abstaining from them … Furthermore, the sages have said that the reward for controlling one's desires is commensurate with the pain involved with doing so, and said, "The gain is according to the pain."

What's more, the sages have enjoined us to desire sin: A person should not say "I have no desire for this sin, even if it were not forbidden by the Torah"... a person should not say, "I have no desire for meat and milk together, I have no desire to wear forbidden mixtures, I have no desire for forbidden relations." Rather, a person should say, "I desire all these things, yet what can I do if my Father in heaven has forbidden it to me."

Celebrating Struggle

Pain with Purpose

TEXT 5A

Rabbi Shneur Zalman of Liadi, Tanya, ch. 2

Rabbi Shneur Zalman of Liadi
(Alter Rebbe)
1745–1812

Chasidic rebbe, halachic authority, and founder of the Chabad movement. The Alter Rebbe was born in Liozna, Belarus, and was among the principal students of the Magid of Mezeritch. His numerous works include the *Tanya*, an early classic containing the fundamentals of Chabad Chasidism, and *Shulchan Aruch HaRav*, an expanded and reworked code of Jewish law.

ואם העצבות אינה מדאגת עונות, אלא מהרהורים רעים ותאוות רעות שנופלות במחשבתו הנה אם נופלות לו שלא בשעת העבודה, אלא בעת עסקו בעסקיו ודרך ארץ וכהאי גוונא אדרבה יש לו לשמוח בחלקו, שאף שנופלות לו במחשבתו הוא מסיח דעתו מהם לקיים מה שנאמר: ולא תתורו אחרי לבבכם ואחרי עיניכם אשר אתם זונים אחריהם ואין הכתוב מדבר בצדיקים לקראם זונים, חס ושלום אלא בבינונים כיוצא בו שנופלים לו הרהורי ניאוף במחשבתו, בין בהיתר כו' וכשמסיח דעתו, מקיים לאו זה ואמרו רז"ל: ישב ולא עבר עבירה, נותנים לו שכר כאילו עשה מצוה ועל כן צריך לשמוח בקיום הלאו כמו בקיום מצות עשה ממש.

If, however, his sadness [stems] from the fact that sinful thoughts and desires enter his mind, then [know this]:

If these thoughts occur to him not during his service of G‑d, but while he is occupied with his own affairs and with mundane matters and the like, he should, on the contrary, be happy in his lot; for although these sinful thoughts enter his mind, he averts his attention from them.

By averting his mind from sinful thoughts, he fulfills the injunction, "You shall not follow after your heart and after your eyes, by which you go astray."

The verse surely does not speak of tzaddikim, *referring to them (G-d forbid) as "going astray," but of* beinonim *like himself, in whose mind there do enter erotic thoughts, whether of an innocent nature [or otherwise], and when he averts his mind from them, he fulfills this injunction. Our sages have said, "When one passively abstains from sin, he is rewarded as though he had actively performed a mitzvah."*

A Different Kind of Mitzvah

TEXT 5B

Ibid.

הרי זאת היא מדת הבינונים ועבודתם לכבוש היצר וההרהור העולה
מהלב למוח, ולהסיח דעתו לגמרי ממנו ולדחותו בשתי ידים, כנ"ל
ובכל דחיה ודחיה שמדחהו ממחשבתו, אתכפיא סטרא אחרא
לתתא ובאתערותא דלתתא אתערותא דלעילא ואתכפיא סטרא
אחרא דלעילא המגביה עצמה כנשר לקיים מה שכתוב: אם תגביה
כנשר וגו' משם אורידך נאם ה' וכמו שהפליג בזהר פרשת תרומה
דף קכח בגודל נחת רוח לפניו יתברך כד אתכפיא סטרא אחרא
לתתא דאסתלק יקרא דקודשא בריך הוא לעילא על כולא יתיר
משבחא אחרא, ואסתלקותא דא יתיר מכולא וכו' ולכן אל יפול לב
אדם עליו ולא ירע לבבו מאד גם אם יהיה כן כל ימיו במלחמה זו כי
אולי לכך נברא, וזאת עבודתו: לאכפיא לסטרא אחרא תמיד

This is the due measure of the beinonim *and their task:
To subdue the evil impulse and the thought that rises
from the heart to the mind, and to completely avert his
mind from it, repulsing it as it were with both hands, as
explained above in [Tanya], ch. 12.*

*With every repulsion of this thought from his mind,
evil is suppressed here below in this world. Inasmuch
as "The arousal from below produces a corresponding
arousal above," evil above in the supernal worlds (the
root of evil of this world)… is also suppressed…*

Indeed the Zohar… extolls the divine satisfaction that occurs when evil is subdued here below, for "Thereby G‑d's glory rises above all, more than by any other praise, and this ascent is greater than all else, etc."

Thus, it is the evil thoughts that enter the mind of the beinoni *that enable him to fulfill G‑d's command in averting his attention from them, thereby subduing evil. Therefore, one should not feel depressed or very troubled at heart, even if he be engaged all his days in this conflict with the thoughts that will always enter his mind. For perhaps this is what he was created for, and this is the service demanded of him—to constantly subdue evil.*

Desiring Desire

TEXT 6

Bamidbar, 11:4

וְהָאסַפְסֻף אֲשֶׁר בְּקִרְבּוֹ הִתְאַוּוּ תַּאֲוָה וַיָּשֻׁבוּ וַיִּבְכּוּ גַּם בְּנֵי יִשְׂרָאֵל וַיֹּאמְרוּ מִי יַאֲכִלֵנוּ בָּשָׂר:

But the multitude among them began to have strong cravings [התאוו תאוה]. Then even the Children of Israel once again began to cry, and they said, "Who will feed us meat?

TEXT 7

Rabbi Yehudah Leib Alter of Gur,
Sefat Emet al HaTorah, Parshat Behaalotecha

ברש"י מי יאכילנו בשר והלא הי' להם מקנה רב רק שמבקשין
עלילה. וקשה מאי עלילה יש מאחר שה' להם. אך יש לומר דכתיב
התאוו תאוה. ומשמע שלא היה להם תאוה. שהוי למעלה מהטבע.
חירות מיצר הרע. ולכך היה נראה להם שנכון שיהיה להם תאוה
ושיזכו לעשות נחת רוח להשם יתברך על ידי שיאכלו בקדושה אף
בשר גשמי.

Rabbi Yehudah
Aryeh Leib Alter
(Sefat Emet)
1847–1905

Chasidic master and scholar.
Rabbi Yehudah Aryeh Leib
Alter assumed the leadership
of the Chasidic dynasty of
Gur (Gora), a town near
Warsaw, Poland, at the age
of 23. He was the grandson
and successor of Rabbi
Yitzchak Meir of Gur, the
founder of the Gur dynasty.
He is commonly referred to
as the *Sefat Emet*, after the
title of his commentaries
on the Torah and Talmud.

On the verse, "Who will feed us meat?" Rashi asked, "But doesn't the verse say, 'Also a great mixed multitude went up with them, and flocks and cattle?'"

But what kind of pretext could this have been, if they in fact did have flocks? The answer is that the verse says התאוו תאוה—*this can be read as, "They desired a desire."*

In other words, they lacked desire, for they were above nature and had freedom from the evil inclination. Therefore, it seemed appropriate to them to desire, so as to merit bringing pleasure to G-d by eating physical meat in a holy fashion.

Playing it Safe

TEXT 8

Talmud Tractate Sanhedrin, 107a

אמר רב יהודה אמר רב לעולם אל יביא אדם עצמו לידי נסיון שהרי
דוד מלך ישראל הביא עצמו לידי נסיון ונכשל אמר לפניו רבונו של
עולם מפני מה אומרים אלקי אברהם אלקי יצחק ואלקי יעקב ואין
אומרים אלקי דוד?

אמר אינהו מינסו לי ואת לא מינסית לי.

אמר לפניו רבונו של עולם בחנני ונסני שנאמר "בחנני ה' ונסני וגו'".
אמר מינסנא לך ועבידנא מילתא בהדך דלדידהו לא הודעתינהו
ואילו אנא קא מודענא לך דמנסינא לך בדבר ערוה... ויתהלך על
גג בית המלך וירא אשה רוחצת מעל הגג והאשה טובת מראה...
וישלח דוד וידרוש לאשה ויאמר הלא זאת בת שבע בת אליעם
אשת אוריה החתי וישלח דוד מלאכים ויקחה ותבא אליו וישכב
עמה... ותשב אל ביתה והיינו דכתיב בחנת לבי פקדת לילה צרפתני
בל תמצא זמותי בל יעבר פי אמר איכו זממא נפל בפומיה דמאן
דסני לי ולא אמר כי הא מילתא.

Rav Yehudah says that Rav says: A person should never bring himself to undergo an ordeal, as David, king of Israel, brought himself to undergo an ordeal and failed.

David said before G-d: Master of the Universe, for what reason does one say in prayer, "G-d of Abraham,

G-d of Isaac, and G-d of Jacob, and one does not say: G-d of David?"

G-d said to David, "They have undergone ordeals before Me, and you have not undergone an ordeal before Me."

David said before Him, "Examine me and subject me to an ordeal, as it is stated, 'Examine me, G-d, and subject me to an ordeal; try my kidneys and my heart.'"

G-d said to him, "I will subject you to an ordeal, and I will perform a matter for you that I did not perform for the Patriarchs, as for them, I did not inform them of the nature of the ordeal, while I am informing you that I will subject you to an ordeal involving a matter of a married woman, with whom relations are forbidden…"

The verse states, "And David walked upon the roof of the king's house; from the roof he saw a woman bathing, and the woman was very fair to look upon" … It is written further, "And David sent and inquired after the woman. And one said: Is not this Bathsheba, daughter of Eliam, the wife of Uriah the Hittite? And David sent messengers, and took her, and she came to him, and he lay with her… and then she returned to her house."

And that is the meaning of the verse, "You have proved my heart; You have visited me in the night: You have tried me, but You find nothing; let no presumptuous thought pass my lips." David said: Oh, that a muzzle would have fallen upon the mouth of the one who hates me, [a euphemism for his own mouth], and I would not have said anything like that and I would have withstood the ordeal.

Siddur
The siddur is the Jewish prayer book. It was originally developed by the sages of the Great Assembly in the 4th century BCE, and later reconstructed by Rabban Gamliel after the destruction of the Second Temple. Various authorities continued to add prayers, from then until contemporary times. It includes praise of G-d, requests for personal and national needs, selections of the Bible, and much else. Various Jewish communities have slightly different versions of the siddur.

TEXT 9

Siddur Tehillat Hashem, Morning Prayer

ואל תביאנו לא לידי נסיון ולא לידי בזיון.

[May it be Your Will, Lord our G-d and G-d of our fathers…] do not bring us to a trial or to a disgrace.

Two Parts of the Second Commandment

TEXT 10

Shemot (Exodus) 20:4

לֹא תִשְׁתַּחֲוֶה לָהֶם וְלֹא תָעָבְדֵם כִּי אָנֹכִי ה' אֱלֹקֶיךָ אֵ-ל קַנָּא פֹּקֵד עֲוֹן אָבֹת עַל בָּנִים עַל שִׁלֵּשִׁים וְעַל רִבֵּעִים לְשֹׂנְאָי:

You shall neither prostrate yourself before them [other gods] nor worship them, for I, the Lord, your G-d, am a zealous G-d, who visits the iniquity of the fathers

upon the sons, upon the third and the fourth generation of those who hate Me.

TEXT 11

Rabbi Mordechai Yosef Leiner of Ishbitza, Mei Hashiloach, Yitro 13

"לא תשתחוה להם ולא תעבדם וגו'". לא תשתחוה היינו שלא תהיה
כפוף תחת איזה דבר שהוא מתנגד לרצונו יתברך רק תתגבר על
כל אלו הדברים שהם כחות זרים ותשוקות זרות, ולא תעבדם שלא
תעשה מהם עבודה להשם יתברך בהכניסך לנסיון כדי שתתגבר
על יצרך ובזה תעבוד השם יתברך על זה בא האזהרה לא תעבדם.

*"You shall neither prostrate yourself before them [other
gods] nor worship them." "Do not prostrate yourself"
refers to anything that is contrary to what G-d wants.
G-d commands us to overcome the challenge of our
inner urges. But "Do not bow down to them" means
we shouldn't make our inclinations into a worship for
Him, i.e., we shouldn't try to evoke our desires and then
try to overcome them and thus serve G-d in that way.*

TEXT 12

Talmud Tractate Sanhedrin, 17a-b

רבי חנינא ורבי יונתן הוו קאזלי באורחא מטו להנהו תרי שבילי חד
פצי אפיתחא דעבודת כוכבים וחד פצי אפיתחא דבי זונות אמר
ליה חד לחבריה ניזיל אפיתחא דעבודת כוכבים דנכיס יצריה אמר
ליה אידך ניזיל אפיתחא דבי זונות ונכפייה ליצרין ונקבל אגרא כי
מטו התם חזינהו [לזונות] איתכנעו מקמייהו אמר ליה מנא לך הא
אמר ליה "מזמה תשמור עלך תבונה תנצרכה".

*Rabbi Chanina and Rabbi Yonatan were once walking
along the road when they came to a certain two paths,
one of which branched off toward the entrance of a
place of idol worship, and the other one branched off
toward the entrance of a brothel.*

*One said to the other, "Let us go by the path that
leads to the entrance of the place of idol worship, as
the inclination to engage in idol worship has been
slaughtered, and the temptation to sin in this manner
no longer exists."*

*The other said to him, "Let us go by the path that
leads to the entrance of the brothel and overpower our
inclination, and thereby receive a reward."*

*When they arrived there, they saw that the prostitutes
yielded before their presence, i.e., they entered the*

building out of respect for the sages. One said to the other, "From where did you know this that the prostitutes would retreat from us in embarrassment?"

He said to him: It is written, "From lewdness [mezimma] it shall watch over you; discernment shall guard you," i.e., the Torah will serve as a safeguard against lewdness.

TEXT 13

Mei Hashiloach, Ibid.

מזה מוכח שאדם אסור להכניס עצמו בנסיון ואפילו אם מכוין שעל ידי זה יתרבה כבוד שמים בהתגברו על היצר וזה הוא לא תעבדם, ושאני רבי חנינא ורבי יונתן שהיו בטוחים שהדברי תורה שיש בהם תשמור אותם.

This story proves that one is not permitted to bring oneself to a test, even if the intention is to overcome it and thus glorify heaven. As for Rabbi Chanina and Rabbi Yonatan, they were on a different plane for they could rely on the merit of their Torah study to protect them.

An Impressive Feat?

TEXT 14

The Lubavitcher Rebbe, Torat Menachem 5719, vol. 2, p. 8

Rabbi Menachem Mendel Schneerson
1902–1994

The towering Jewish leader of the 20th century, known as "the Lubavitcher Rebbe," or simply as "the Rebbe." Born in southern Ukraine, the Rebbe escaped Nazi-occupied Europe, arriving in the U.S. in June 1941. The Rebbe inspired and guided the revival of traditional Judaism after the European devastation, impacting virtually every Jewish community the world over. The Rebbe often emphasized that the performance of just one additional good deed could usher in the era of Mashiach. The Rebbe's scholarly talks and writings have been printed in more than 200 volumes.

על הפסוק "ויקהל משה את כל עדת בני ישראל" איתא בזהר "אלין גוברין, דכניש לון ואפריש לון לחודייהו". והיינו שמדייק מלשון "עדת בני ישראל", בני ישראל ולא בנות ישראל. ומבאר בזה האור החיים הקדוש "ומן הסתם לא יכחיש שלא נזדמנו הנשים ... אלא יכוון לומר כי הקהיל האנשים בפני עצמן והנשים בפני עצמן". והטעם שהוצרכו להיות האנשים בפני עצמם והנשים בפני עצמן ... כדי למנוע נסיונות כו'.

ההוראה מענין זה: ישנם אלו שרצונם להראות "קונצן", ומכניסים עצמם בנסיונות, בטענה שכאשר אין להם נסיונות אין כל "קונץ" בכך שהנהגתם היא כדבעי ... ולכן—טוענים הם—יש צורך ללכת למקומות כו', ואף על פי כן להימנע מענינים שאינם כדבעי, ואזי יהי' זה "קונץ"! ... —כ"ק מו"ח אדמו"ר דיבר פעם אודות מי שטוען: וכי "קונץ" הוא לשבת בבית-המדרש? צריכים ללכת ברחוב, ושם להתנהג כדבעי! וממשיך—וכי קונץ הוא ללכת ברחוב בלבד? יש ללכת לתיאטראות כו', ושם להתאפק מלנהוג שלא כראוי, ובכך יראה את "גבורתו"—"איזהו גיבור הכובש את יצרו"! וגם בכך אינו מסתפק, אלא הולך למקומות האסורים משום צניעות כו'; וגם בכך לא די לו, אלא רצונו לנהוג כדברי הגמרא בנוגע לענין התשובה, שצ"ל "באותה אשה באותו פרק כו'" ...

והמענה לזה—שאין זקוקים ל"קונצן" שלהם! כל אחד ואחד מישראל מבקש מהקב"ה "ואל תביאנו לידי נסיון", ועל אחת כמה וכמה שאסור לאדם להביא עצמו לידי נסיון! וכפי שמצינו אפילו בדוד המלך ש"הביא עצמו לידי נסיון ונכשל", ובוודאי שאין תובעים ממנו שיהי' גדול

מדוד המלך . . . די לו אם יהי' מדריגה אחת למטה מדוד המלך! . . .
וזוהי ההוראה מפרשתנו: כשהי' צורך להקהיל את ישראל למטרת
בנין המשכן . . . שזוהי מטרה היותר נעלית, תכלית הכוונה של
כל ההשתלשלות, ונוסף לזה היתה ההקהלה על ידי משה רבינו,
וזמן ההקהלה הי' למחרת יום הכיפורים, שבו דומין בני ישראל
למלאכים כו'—הנה לאחרי כל זה, הוצרכו להבטיח שלא להקהיל
אנשים ונשים יחד. ומכאן הוראה לכל הזמנים: כאשר מתאספים
יחד, לאיזו מטרה שתהי', ולו הקדושה ביותר—אסור להביא עצמם
לידי נסיונות, ודוקא על ידי הנהגה זו אפשר לגשת לקיום הענין
ד"ושכנתי בתוכם".

On the verse, "And Moses gathered the entire congregation of the Children of Israel," the Zohar states, "This
refers to the men, for Moshe spoke to them separately."
The Zohar infers from the word "bnei—the sons—of
Israel" that the verse refers to the sons of Israel and not
to the daughters of Israel.

But the Ohr Hachaim explains that this doesn't mean
Moses spoke only to the men and not to the women,
rather that Moses gathered the men separately and the
women separately. The reason was to avoid temptation, etc.

The lesson is: Some people want to do "tricks" and put
themselves into tempting situations, with the attitude
that without temptation, it's no big deal to do the right
thing. Therefore, they claim, it is necessary to go to
tempting places, etc., and to refrain even there from

forbidden behavior—and that, *they believe, will be an impressive feat.*

My father-in-law, the Rebbe, once spoke about a person who says, "What is so impressive about sitting in the study hall? Rather, we must go out in the street, and even there act appropriately." Then he takes it a step further and says, "What is so impressive about just going in the street? Better to go to the theaters, etc., and refrain even there from inappropriate behavior, and this will demonstrate true 'strength,' for after all, the Mishnah says, 'Who is strong? He who conquers his evil inclination.'" And then this person takes it a step further, and even goes to places that are forbidden by the laws of modesty, etc., and even that is not enough—he wishes to behave in the way the Talmud talks about repentance, that true repentance is when one finds himself "with the same woman, at the same time, etc."

The response to this attitude is: Nobody needs such "impressive" feats! Each and every Jew asks G-d "not to bring me to a test," and certainly it is forbidden for one to place himself in a tempting situation. As we find regarding King David, who "brought himself to a test and failed." Certainly we are not expected to be greater than King David ... after all, it's fine if a person is a notch lower than King David!

This, then, is the lesson: Even when there is a need to gather Jews for building the Mishkan, *which is the highest purpose, the purpose of all creation, and what's more, the gathering is done by Moshe, on the day after Yom Kippur, when we are all like angels—nevertheless, it was necessary not to gather the men and women together. This is a lesson for all times: When Jews gather together for whatever purpose, it is forbidden for them to enter into tempting situations. Specifically with this approach it is possible to bring the Divine Presence into our midst.*

9

SHELACH

Man of the People

How One Man Stemmed a Revolution and Won Over a Nation

PARSHAH OVERVIEW
Shelach

Moses sends twelve spies to the land of Canaan. Forty days later they return, carrying a huge cluster of grapes, a pomegranate, and a fig, to report on a lush and bountiful land. But ten of the spies warn that the inhabitants of the land are giants and warriors "more powerful than we"; only Caleb and Joshua insist that the land can be conquered, as G-d has commanded.

The people weep that they'd rather return to Egypt. G-d decrees that Israel's entry into the Land shall be delayed forty years, during which time that entire generation will die out in the desert. A group of remorseful Jews storm the mountain on the border of the Land, and are routed by the Amalekites and Canaanites.

The laws of the menachot *(meal, wine, and oil offerings) are given, as well as the mitzvah to consecrate a portion of the dough (challah) to G-d when making bread. A man violates the Shabbat by gathering sticks, and is put to death. G-d instructs to place fringes (tzitzit) on the four corners of our garments, so that we should remember to fulfill the mitzvot (divine commandments).*

Stemming the Tide

The Spies

TEXT 1A

Bamidbar (Numbers) 13:16

אֵלֶּה שְׁמוֹת הָאֲנָשִׁים אֲשֶׁר שָׁלַח מֹשֶׁה לָתוּר אֶת הָאָרֶץ וַיִּקְרָא מֹשֶׁה
לְהוֹשֵׁעַ בִּן נוּן יְהוֹשֻׁעַ:

These are the names of the men Moses sent to scout the Land, and Moses called Hoshea the son of Nun, Joshua.

TEXT 1B

Rashi, ad. loc

Rabbi Shlomo Yitzchaki
(Rashi)
1040–1105
Most noted biblical and Talmudic commentator. Born in Troyes, France, Rashi studied in the famed *yeshivot* of Mainz and Worms. His commentaries on the Pentateuch and the Talmud, which focus on the straightforward meaning of the text, appear in virtually every edition of the Talmud and Bible.

"ויקרא משה להושע וגו'". התפלל עליו י-ה יושיעך מעצת מרגלים.

"And Moses called Hoshea … " He prayed on his behalf, "May G-d save you from the counsel of the spies." [The name יְהוֹשֻׁעַ *is a compounded form of* יָ-ה יוֹשִׁיעֲךָ, *May G-d save you.]*

TEXT 2A

Bamidbar (Numbers) 13:22

וַיַּעֲלוּ בַנֶּגֶב וַיָּבֹא עַד חֶבְרוֹן וְשָׁם אֲחִימַן שֵׁשַׁי וְתַלְמַי יְלִידֵי הָעֲנָק וְחֶבְרוֹן שֶׁבַע שָׁנִים נִבְנְתָה לִפְנֵי צֹעַן מִצְרָיִם:

They went up in the south, and he came to Hebron, and there were Ahiman, Sheshai, and Talmai, the descendants of the giant. Now Hebron had been built seven years before Zoan of Egypt.

TEXT 2B

Rashi, ad. loc

"וַיָּבֹא עַד חֶבְרוֹן". כלב לבדו הלך שם ונשתטח על קברי אבות, שלא יהא ניסת לחבריו להיות בעצתם, וכן הוא אומר "ולו אתן את הארץ אשר דרך בה", וכתיב "ויתנו לכלב את חברון".

"And he came to Hebron." Caleb went there alone [hence the singular "he came"] to prostrate himself on the graves of the Patriarchs [in prayer] that he not be enticed by his colleagues to be part of their counsel. Thus, it says, "I will give him [Caleb] the land on which he has walked," and it is written, "They gave Hebron to Caleb."

The Spies Return

TEXT 3

Bamidbar (Numbers) 13:27-29

וַיְסַפְּרוּ לוֹ וַיֹּאמְרוּ בָּאנוּ אֶל הָאָרֶץ אֲשֶׁר שְׁלַחְתָּנוּ וְגַם זָבַת חָלָב וּדְבַשׁ
הִוא וְזֶה פִּרְיָהּ.
אֶפֶס כִּי עַז הָעָם הַיֹּשֵׁב בָּאָרֶץ וְהֶעָרִים בְּצֻרוֹת גְּדֹלֹת מְאֹד וְגַם יְלִדֵי
הָעֲנָק רָאִינוּ שָׁם.
עֲמָלֵק יוֹשֵׁב בְּאֶרֶץ הַנֶּגֶב וְהַחִתִּי וְהַיְבוּסִי וְהָאֱמֹרִי יוֹשֵׁב בָּהָר וְהַכְּנַעֲנִי
יוֹשֵׁב עַל הַיָּם וְעַל יַד הַיַּרְדֵּן.

They told him and said, "We came to the land to which you sent us, and it is flowing with milk and honey, and this is its fruit.

"However, the people who inhabit the land are mighty, and the cities are extremely huge and fortified, and there we saw even the offspring of the giant.

"The Amalekites dwell in the south land, while the Hittites, the Jebusites, and the Amorites dwell in the mountainous region. The Canaanites dwell on the coast and alongside the Jordan."

TEXT 4A

Ibid., v. 30-31

וַיַּהַס כָּלֵב אֶת הָעָם אֶל מֹשֶׁה; וַיֹּאמֶר עָלֹה נַעֲלֶה וְיָרַשְׁנוּ אֹתָהּ כִּי יָכוֹל
נוּכַל לָהּ.

וְהָאֲנָשִׁים אֲשֶׁר עָלוּ עִמּוֹ אָמְרוּ לֹא נוּכַל לַעֲלוֹת אֶל הָעָם כִּי חָזָק
הוּא מִמֶּנּוּ.

Caleb silenced the people to [hear about] Moses, and he said, "We can surely go up and take possession of it, for we can indeed overcome it."

But the men who went up with him said, "We are unable to go up against the people, for they are stronger than we."

TEXT 4B

Rashi, ad. loc

אל משה. לשמוע מה שידבר במשה, צווח ואמר, וכי זו בלבד עשה
לנו בן עמרם, השומע היה סבור שבא לספר בגנותו, ומתוך שהיה
בלבם על משה בשביל דברי המרגלים שתקו כלם לשמוע גנותו,
אמר, והלא קרע לנו את הים והוריד לנו את המן והגיז לנו את השליו.

*"To Moses." To hear what he would say about Moses.
He cried out, "Is this the only thing the son of Amram
has done to us?" Anyone listening might have thought
that he intended to disparage him, and because there
was [resentment] in their hearts against Moses because
of the spies' report, they all became silent so they could
hear his defamation. But he said, "Didn't he split the
sea for us, bring down the manna for us, and cause the
quails to fly down to us?"*

TEXT 4C

Ibid.

"עלה נעלה". אפילו בשמים, והוא אומר עשו סולמות ועלו שם,
נצליח בכל דבריו.

*"We can surely go up." Even if Moses would tell us
to make ladders to ascend to the heavens, we would
be successful.*

Man of Struggle

"My Servant Caleb"

TEXT 5

Bamidbar (Numbers) 14:24

וְעַבְדִּי כָלֵב עֵקֶב הָיְתָה רוּחַ אַחֶרֶת עִמּוֹ וַיְמַלֵּא אַחֲרָי וַהֲבִיאֹתִיו אֶל הָאָרֶץ אֲשֶׁר בָּא שָׁמָּה וְזַרְעוֹ יוֹרִשֶׁנָּה.

But as for My servant Caleb, because he was possessed by another spirit, and he followed Me, I will bring him to the land to which he came, and his descendants will drive it[s inhabitants] out.

TEXT 6

Devarim (Deuteronomy) 1:36

זוּלָתִי כָּלֵב בֶּן יְפֻנֶּה הוּא יִרְאֶנָּה וְלוֹ אֶתֵּן אֶת הָאָרֶץ אֲשֶׁר דָּרַךְ בָּהּ וּלְבָנָיו יַעַן אֲשֶׁר מִלֵּא אַחֲרֵי ה'.

Except Caleb the son of Jephunneh. He will see it, and I will give him the land he trod upon, and to his children, because he has completely followed G-d.

TEXT 7A

Rabbi Chayim ibn Atar, Or Hachayim to Bamidbar 14:24

Rabbi Chayim ibn Atar
(*Or Hachayim*)
1696–1743

Biblical exegete, kabbalist,
and Talmudist. Rabbi Atar,
born in Meknes, Morocco, was
a prominent member of the
Moroccan rabbinate and later
immigrated to the Land of
Israel. He is most famous for
his *Or Hachayim*, a popular
commentary on the Torah. The
famed Jewish historian and
bibliophile Rabbi Chaim Yosef
David Azulai was among
his most notable disciples.

"וְעַבְדִּי כָלֵב עֵקֶב וְגוֹ'". צריך לדעת למה לא הזכיר אלא כלב ולא
יהושע, גם כוונת אומרו היתה רוח אחרת עמו?

"And My servant Caleb." It is puzzling, why is only
Caleb is mentioned and not Joshua? The words, *"Possessed by another spirit"* are also puzzling, what is the
meaning of this unique phrase?

Caleb's Struggles

TEXT 7B

Ibid.

אכן פירוש הכתוב הוא ועבדי כלב טעם שאני קורא אותו עבדי הוא
עקב פירוש שכר אשר היתה רוח אחרת עמו . . . כלב שנכנס בגדר
סכנת יצר הרע וחברתו הרשעה ותחל רוח רעה לפעמו, והראיה
שהלך ונשתטח על קברות האבות, והוא אומרו רוח אחרת עמו ואף
על פי כן וימלא אחרי פירוש השלים אחר רצונו יתברך.
ודקדק לומר בדרך זה לצד שיש באדם ב' יועצין יועץ רע ויועץ
טוב ללכת אחרי ה' והוא השלים ומילא אחרי חלק ה', וזה הוא
על דרך אומרם ז"ל "מי שבאה עבירה לידו וניצול ממנה נותנין לו
שכר כעושה מצוה", וזה אינו ביהושע כי לא היתה רוח אחרת עמו
להטעותו מדרך השכל כי משה מנעו. אשר על כן זכה כלב שיקרא
עבד ה' כמשה רבינו עליו השלום.

What is intended with the words that Caleb "possessed another spirit," is that the very reason why he is deserving reward is because he possessed a spirit that can be labeled "other."... Caleb was at risk of being tempted by his base urges. Along with that, the negative influence of his peers caused a negative ["other"] spirit to rouse within him. Proof of this is the fact that he went to prostrate himself on the graves of the Patriarchs. This, then is what is intended with the words, "another spirit" [i.e., a negative spirit]. Nevertheless, "And he followed Me," namely, he followed the will of G-d [as opposed to his own personal inclination.] The verse uses this precise language inasmuch as there are two councils within every person—a negative one advocating evil, and a positive one advocating goodness and walking in the ways of G-d. Caleb chose the latter. G-d's reaction is in line with the Talmud's statement that "one who has the chance to commit a sin and is spared therefrom receives reward as though he had performed a mitzvah." Joshua did not have this quality, for he did not possess an opposing spirit, seeking to sway him from the intelligent path, for Moses had prevented that. Thus, Caleb merited the title, "Servant of G-d," akin to Moses, peace unto him.

A Three-Pronged Message of Hope

A Three-Part Challenge

TEXT 8

Bamidbar (Numbers) 13:28-29

אֶפֶס כִּי עַז הָעָם הַיּשֵׁב בָּאָרֶץ וְהֶעָרִים בְּצֻרוֹת גְּדֹלֹת מְאֹד וְגַם יְלִדֵי הָעֲנָק רָאִינוּ שָׁם:

עֲמָלֵק יוֹשֵׁב בְּאֶרֶץ הַנֶּגֶב וְהַחִתִּי וְהַיְבוּסִי וְהָאֱמֹרִי יוֹשֵׁב בָּהָר וְהַכְּנַעֲנִי יֹשֵׁב עַל הַיָּם וְעַל יַד הַיַּרְדֵּן:

However, the people who inhabit the land are mighty, and the cities are extremely huge and fortified, and there we saw even the offspring of the giant. The Amalekites dwell in the south land, while the Hittites, the Jebusites, and the Amorites dwell in the mountainous region. The Canaanites dwell on the coast and alongside the Jordan.

Believing in Yourself

TEXT 9

Yalkut Shimoni, Beshalach 261

כשיצאו ישראל ממצרים הקיפם הקדוש ברוך ה' בז' ענני כבוד,
שנאמר, "יסובבנהו יבוננהו".
בקשו מן נתן להם. כיון שנתן להם כל צרכיהם, התחילו מהרהרים
ואומרים: היש ה' בקרבנו? אמר להם הקדוש ברוך הוא: הרהרתם
עלי, חייכם, שאני מודיע לכם, הרי הכלב בא ונושך אתכם. ואי זה?
זה עמלק, שנאמר, "ויבא עמלק".

Yalkut Shimoni
A Midrash that covers the
entire biblical text. Its material
is collected from all over
rabbinic literature, including
the Babylonian and Jerusalem
Talmuds and various ancient
Midrashic texts. It contains
several passages from
Midrashim that have been lost,
as well as different versions
of existing *Midrashim*. It is
unclear when and by whom
this Midrash was redacted.

*When the Jews left Egypt, G-d surrounded them with
seven clouds of glory.*

*They asked for manna, and it was granted. After all
their needs had been met, they started wondering and
mused, "Is there a G-d among us?" G-d replied, "You
doubted me? I swear on your lives that you will need
Me—the dog will come and bite you." Who is that dog?
—Amalek, as the verse states, "And Amalek came."*

Caleb's Response

TEXT 10

Likutei Sichot, vol. 8, p. 88

Rabbi Menachem Mendel Schneerson
1902–1994

The towering Jewish leader of the 20th century, known as "the Lubavitcher Rebbe," or simply as "the Rebbe." Born in southern Ukraine, the Rebbe escaped Nazi-occupied Europe, arriving in the U.S. in June 1941. The Rebbe inspired and guided the revival of traditional Judaism after the European devastation, impacting virtually every Jewish community the world over. The Rebbe often emphasized that the performance of just one additional good deed could usher in the era of Mashiach. The Rebbe's scholarly talks and writings have been printed in more than 200 volumes.

אויף זייער טענה "עז העם היושב בארץ גו' ", האט ער געענטפערט: "קרע לנו את הים" אויך ביי קריעת ים סוף האט געדארפט זיין א מלחמה וואס על פי טבע האבן זיי ניט געקענט מנצח זיין...

אויף זייער טענה "עמלק יושב בארץ הנגב", האט ער געענטפערט "הגיז לנו את השליו": אויך די טענה "מי יאכילנו בשר" איז געווען בלויז "שמבקשים עלילה" און פונדעסטוועגן—"הגיז לנו את השליו".

און אויף דער טענה "והחתי והיבוסי גו' ועל יד הירדן" איז געווען זיין ענטפער צו זיי "הוריד לנו את המן": אויך דער מן וואס איז געווען אין מדבר, איז געווען ניט קיין ענין עיקרי — די גאנצע הליכה במדבר איז דאך געווען בלויז א הכנה אויף אנקומען אין ארץ ישראל, און פונדעסטוועגן "הוריד לנו את המן" — איז דאך דערפון געדרונגען, אז דער אויבערשטער וועט מאכן ניסים אויך אויפן וועג.

In response to the spies' claim that "the people who inhabit the land are mighty," Caleb responded that by the splitting of the sea, the situation also called for a war that was naturally unwinnable…

In response to the claim, "Amalek dwells in the south," Caleb responded, "He caused the quails to fly down to us": The Jews complaint, "Who will feed us meat?" [which brought about the quail] was also just them making trouble, and nevertheless, G-d responded and "rained down quail."

In response to their claim, "The Hittites, the Jebusites… on the side of the Jordan," Caleb evoked the man: *The entire sojourn of the Jews in the desert was a technical, auxiliary thing—a path to get to Israel. Nevertheless, G-d still provided the Jews with* man—*clear proof that G-d provides miracles even for matters that are only "on the way" to the goal.*

Caleb the Inspiration

TEXT 11

Likutei Sichot, Ibid.

אויף דעם קומט די הוראה פון כלב'ן: כלב אליין האט מורא געהאט "שלא יהא ניסת לחבריו להיות בעצתם". און פונדעסטוועגן האט ער ניט אפגעלאזן די שליחות אין וועלכער משה האט אים געשיקט, נאר "נשתטח על קברי אבות" (בדרך העלאה מלמטה למעלה— דורך זיין עבודה), און דורך דעם האט ער גע'פועל'ט' אז ניט נאר איז ער ניצול געווארן פון עצת המרגלים, נאר אויך "השתיק את כולם"—ער האך מהפך געווען אפילו די מרגלים, אז אויך זיי האבן זיך צוגעהערט צו זיינע רייד "עלה נעלה וירשנו אותה".

און דורך דער הנהגה ניט צו נתפעל ווערן פון קיין שום שוועריקייטן, זיך ניט רעכענען מיט קיינע חשבונות

און אנגיין מיט דער ארבעט צו מאכן די גאנצע וועלט פאר א
מקום תורה — "ארץ ישראל" (ברוחניות) — וועט מען זוכה זיין
צום קיום היעוד "עתידה ארץ ישראל (בגשמיות) שתתפשט בכל
הארצות" . . .

And then comes Caleb's inspiration: Caleb had also
personally feared that he would get swept up in the
spies' plot. Despite that, he did not abandon the mission Moses charged him with and instead went to pray
at the graves of the Patriarcs. By so doing, not only
did he avoid attaching himself to the spies' plans, he
"silenced everyone"—he transformed the spies to the
extent that they listened to his words, "We will ascend
and inherit the Land."

We ought to emulate such behavior: Not to be impressed
by any challenges, rather to cease all machinations and
simply forge forward in the holy task of transforming
the world into a place of Torah, a spiritual Israel of
sorts. Doing so will certainly bring about the realization of the promise that Israel will spread to all lands
[with the coming of Mashiach].

Tackling Your Inner Spy

TEXT 12

Rabbi Yosef Yitzchak Schneersohn of Lubavitch,
Sefer Hamaamarim 5690, p. 119

דער יצר הרע איז אַ אומן, אַ קינסטלער אויף קאָנען צוגיין צו יעדער
מענטשן לויט זיין מהות און זיין מצב, און די ערשטע אַרבעט פון
דעם יצר הרע איז אַריינצונעמען דעם מענטשען אין האַנט, אין
זיין רשות, אַז דער מענטש זאָל איהם אין אַלעס פאָלגן.
מא. די קונסט פון דעם יצר הרע איז, וואָס ער האָט פאַר יעדער סוג
מענטש אַ שפראַך ווי צוצוגיין צו יעדערן, און געפינט וועגן ווי אַזוי
אַריינצובעקומען דעם מענטשן אין זיין רשות.

Rabbi Yosef Yitzchak Schneersohn
(Rayatz, Frierdiker Rebbe, Previous Rebbe)
1880–1950

Chasidic rebbe, prolific writer, and Jewish activist. Rabbi Yosef Yitzchak, the sixth leader of the Chabad movement, actively promoted Jewish religious practice in Soviet Russia and was arrested for these activities. After his release from prison and exile, he settled in Warsaw, Poland, from where he fled Nazi occupation, and arrived in New York in 1940. Settling in Brooklyn, Rabbi Schneerson worked to revitalize American Jewish life. His son-in law, Rabbi Menachem Mendel Schneersohn, succeeded him as the leader of the Chabad movement.

The yetzer hara *is crafty in the sense that he's able to approach every person and influence him with tailor-made cunningness. The groundwork of the* yetzer hara *is to take the person by the hand, under his influence, and ensure that the person follows him unequivocally.*

The yetzer hara's *trick is that he has suitable language to approach every person individually, finding that exact unique angle of how to win the person over into his dominion.*

TEXT 13

The Lubavitcher Rebbe, Igrot Kodesh, vol. 1, p. 157

א ין היינטיגער סדרה ווערט דאך דערציילט די מעשה פון די
מרגלים, די מרגלים זיינען געווען ראשי בני ישראל ואותה שעה
כשרים היו, אויך דערנאך האבען זיי אנגעהויבען מיט זאגען: זבת
חלב ודבש היא, כי עז העם היושב בארץ גו' עמלק יושב בארץ
הנגב גו'—וואס דאס אלץ איז געווען אמת, נאר דער אויספיר—לא
נוכל לעלות אל העם כי חזק הוא ממנו—איז געווען פאלש און די
גמרא ערקלערט (סוטה לה, א) וואס דאס מיינט: כביכול אפילו
בעל הבית אינו יכול להוציא כליו—כפירה.

ב דוגמא זו, מען טענה'ט אז אין אמעריקע איז זבת חלב ודבש,
מען האט אלע תענוגים גשמיים און מ'איז פארטאן אין זיי, מ'איז
ארומגערינגעלט מיט עמלקים—איז ווי קען מען גאר רעדען מיט
א צווייטען וואס איז ווייט פון יהדות וועגען איינפירען א שטרייגינגען
תורה ומצות לעבען, ניט דא איז דער ארט אויף דעם—איז דאס
ר"ל, היפך האמונה, מען דארף נאר האבען בא זיך דעם החלט, ווי
כלב האט געזאגט: עלה נעלה—וועט במילא זיין יכול נוכל לה.

O ur parshah relates the story of the spies. These spies were heads of Israel and, at the time, were quite righteous. When they returned, they made all sorts of claims, "The nations are fortified … Amalek is there, etc."—claims that were indeed true. The problem was with their conclusion, "We cannot defeat the people for they are stronger than us." This was patently false, as the Talmud states that they reasoned that even G-d could not perform the task—words of outright heresy.

In a similar vein, people claim today that we are now in America, a land flowing with milk and honey and all delectable items, and we are surrounded by Amalek. How can we think of speaking with other Jews who are distanced from Torah and mitzvot about leading a religious life? This is not the place for that!

This is, sadly, the antithesis of faith. We need to only have the inner resolve as Caleb did, "We will surely ascend," and we will, then, be able to do so!

10

Sophisticated Animal?

The Total Is More than Just the Sum of the Parts

PARSHAH OVERVIEW
Korach

Korach incites a mutiny challenging Moses's leadership and the granting of the kehunah *(priesthood) to Aaron. He is accompanied by Moses's inveterate foes, Dathan and Abiram. Joining them are 250 distinguished members of the community, who offer the sacrosanct* ketoret *(incense) to prove their worthiness for the priesthood. The earth opens up and swallows the mutineers, and a fire consumes the* ketoret-*offerers.*

A subsequent plague is stopped by Aaron's offering of ketoret. *Aaron's staff miraculously blossoms and brings forth almonds, to prove that his designation as High Priest is divinely ordained.*

G-d commands that a terumah *("uplifting") from each crop of grain, wine and oil, as well as all firstborn sheep and cattle, and other specified gifts, be given to the* kohanim *(priests).*

Korach's Dissent

Korach and Moshe

TEXT 1

Bamidbar (Numbers) 16:1-3

וַיִּקַּח קֹרַח בֶּן יִצְהָר בֶּן קְהָת בֶּן לֵוִי וְדָתָן וַאֲבִירָם בְּנֵי אֱלִיאָב וְאוֹן בֶּן פֶּלֶת בְּנֵי רְאוּבֵן:

וַיָּקֻמוּ לִפְנֵי מֹשֶׁה וַאֲנָשִׁים מִבְּנֵי יִשְׂרָאֵל חֲמִשִּׁים וּמָאתָיִם נְשִׂיאֵי עֵדָה קְרִאֵי מוֹעֵד אַנְשֵׁי שֵׁם:

וַיִּקָּהֲלוּ עַל מֹשֶׁה וְעַל אַהֲרֹן וַיֹּאמְרוּ אֲלֵהֶם רַב לָכֶם כִּי כָל הָעֵדָה כֻּלָּם קְדֹשִׁים וּבְתוֹכָם ה' וּמַדּוּעַ תִּתְנַשְּׂאוּ עַל קְהַל ה':

Korach, the son of Yitzhar, the son of Kehos, the son of Levi, with Dathan and Abiram, the sons of Eliav, and On, the son of Peles, sons of Reuben, convinced men to join him.

They rose up against Moses, together with other sons of Israel, two hundred and fifty men in total, princes of the congregation, the elect men of the assembly, men of renown.

They assembled themselves together against Moses and Aaron, and said to them, "You take too much for yourselves. The entire congregation are holy, every one of them! G-d is among them. Why, then, do you place yourselves above the congregation of G-d?"

TEXT 2

Ibid., 16:5-7

וַיְדַבֵּר אֶל קֹרַח וְאֶל כָּל עֲדָתוֹ לֵאמֹר בֹּקֶר וְיֹדַע ה' אֶת אֲשֶׁר לוֹ וְאֶת
הַקָּדוֹשׁ וְהִקְרִיב אֵלָיו וְאֵת אֲשֶׁר יִבְחַר בּוֹ יַקְרִיב אֵלָיו:
זֹאת עֲשׂוּ קְחוּ לָכֶם מַחְתּוֹת קֹרַח וְכָל עֲדָתוֹ:
וּתְנוּ בָהֶן אֵשׁ וְשִׂימוּ עֲלֵיהֶן קְטֹרֶת לִפְנֵי ה' מָחָר וְהָיָה הָאִישׁ אֲשֶׁר
יִבְחַר ה' הוּא הַקָּדוֹשׁ רַב לָכֶם בְּנֵי לֵוִי:

And he said to Korach and his whole group, "In the morning, G-d will show who are His, and who is holy, and will draw them close to Him. He will draw close the one whom He has chosen.

"Do this: You, Korach, and all your company, should take incense pans.

"Fill them with fire, and offer incense upon them before G-d tomorrow. Whomever G-d chooses will be holy. This is a great responsibility, sons of Levi."

Korach's Wisdom

TEXT 3

Midrash Bamidbar Rabah, 18:8

Bamidbar Rabah

An exegetical commentary on the first seven chapters of the Book of Numbers and a homiletic commentary on the rest of the book. The first part of *Bamidbar Rabah* is notable for its inclusion of esoteric material; the second half is essentially identical to *Midrash Tanchuma* on the Book of Numbers. It was first printed in Constantinople in 1512, together with four other Midrashic works on the other four books of the Pentateuch.

וקרח שפקח היה — מה ראה לשטות הזה?

If Korach was so wise, how was he open to such foolishness?

Korach Was a Heretic

TEXT 4

Jerusalem Talmud, Tractate Sanhedrin, 10a

רב אמר קרח אפיקרסי היה.

מה עשה? עמד ועשה טלית שכולן תכלת, אתא גבי משה אמר ליה: "משה רבינו, טלית שכולה תכלת מה שתהא חייבת בציצית?" אמר לו: "חייבת, דכתיב 'גדילים תעשה לך וגו'".

"בית שהוא מלא ספרים, מהו שיהא חייב במזוזה?" אמר לו: "חייב במזוזה, דכתיב 'וכתבתם על מזוזות ביתך וגו'". אמר לו: "בהרת כגריס מהו?" אמר לו: "טמא". "פרחה בכולו?" אמר לו: "טהור". באותו שעה אמר קרח: "אין תורה מן השמים, ולא משה נביא, ולא אהרן כהן גדול".

Rav said: Korach was a heretic who challenged Moshe with religious questions. What did he do? He made a tallit entirely out of techeilet *and asked Moshe, our teacher, whether it required* tzitzit *strings on its corners. Moshe replied, "It does require them, as the verse says, you shall make strings."*

Korach then asked Moshe whether a house full of holy scrolls requires a mezuzah. Moshe replied, "It does, as the verse states, 'Write it upon the doorpost.'"

He then asked what the law states regarding a baheret *the size of a bean. Moshe replied, "It is impure." Korach asked the law regarding a* baheret *that spread to cover the entire body. Moshe replied, "It is pure."*

Korach said at that moment, "The Torah is not from heaven, Moshe is not a prophet, and Aharon is not the High Priest.'"

Jerusalem Talmud
A commentary to the Mishnah, compiled during the fourth and fifth centuries. The Jerusalem Talmud predates its Babylonian counterpart by 100 years and is written in both Hebrew and Aramaic. While the Babylonian Talmud is the most authoritative source for Jewish law, the Jerusalem Talmud remains an invaluable source for the spiritual, intellectual, ethical, historical, and legal traditions of Judaism.

Quality–Addition or Transformation?

Common Denominators

TEXT 5

Rabbi Yosef Rosen, The Rogatchover Ga'on,
Tsafnat Pane'ach al HaTorah, Bamidbar 16:3

Rabbi Yosef Rosen
(Rogatchover Gaon)
1858–1936

One of the prominent talmudic scholars of the early 20th century. Born in Rogachev, Belarus, to a Chasidic family, his unusual capabilities were recognized at a young age. At thirteen, he was brought to Slutsk to study with Rabbi Yosef Ber Soloveitchik. He remained there for a full year, studying primarily with the rabbi's son, the legendary Chaim Soloveitchik. Later, he moved on to Shklov, where he studied with Rabbi Moshe Yehoshua Leib Diskin. After a period in Warsaw, the home city of his wife, he assumed the rabbinate of the Chasidic community in Dvinsk, Latvia. His works, titled *Tsafnat Pane'ach*, are famed for both their depth and difficulty.

עיקר הגדר טענת קרח, אם בדבר אשר הגדול והקטן שוים אם גם בזה יש מעלה להגדול על הקטן . . ועל זה חלק קרח – וזה הרמז "למה תתנשאו וכו'" – ואמר דבדבר שהם שוים אין לזה מעלה על זה, ונפקא מינה בכל מעלות אם גם הדבר השוה לא דמו.

Korach's claim was primarily defined by a philosophical question: When a greater and a lesser entity both share a common quality, is the greater entity still greater even in that quality they share? . . . This was Korach's departure from Moshe and the Torah, and is implied by his words, "Why do you place yourself above them?" Korach claimed that in those things he shared with Moshe and Aharon, they were essentially equal. And this claim affects all questions of whether common denominators between unequal parties are truly equal.

Reading the Torah
from a Chumash Scroll

TEXT 6

Talmud Tractate Gittin, 60a

שלחו ליה בני גליל לרבי חלבו: מהו לקרות בחומשים בבית הכנסת
בציבור [שיש שכותבין להן חמשה חומשין כל חומש אחד שלם
לעצמו, וכל ספריהם היו במגילה כספר תורה שלנו, רש"י]?
לא הוה בידיה. אתא שייליה לרב יצחק נפחא, לא הוה בידיה.
אתא שאיל בי מדרשא, ופשטוה מהא דאמר רב שמואל בר נחמני
אמר רב יוחנן: ספר תורה שחסר יריעה אחת – אין קורין בו.
ולא היא; התם מחסר במילתיה [שקורין לו ספר תורה וחסר הוא,
רש"י], הכא לא מחסר במילתיה.

Babylonian Talmud
A literary work of monumental proportions that draws upon the legal, spiritual, intellectual, ethical, and historical traditions of Judaism. The 37 tractates of the Babylonian Talmud contain the teachings of the Jewish sages from the period after the destruction of the Second Temple through the fifth century CE. It has served as the primary vehicle for the transmission of the Oral Law and the education of Jews over the centuries; it is the entry point for all subsequent legal, ethical, and theological Jewish scholarship.

The Galileans sent a question to Rabbi Chelbo: Is it permissible to use an individual Chumash *scroll for the public Torah reading in the synagogue?*

Rabbi Chelbo did not know what to answer. The question reached Rabbi Yitzchak Nafcha, and he, too, did not know what to answer.

He asked the question to the Beit Midrash, *the house of learning, and they found the answer in light of what Rabbi Shmuel bar Nachmeini said in the name of Rabbi Yochanan: One may not read from a Torah scroll missing even one panel of parchment. So how* can one read from a single Chumash, *which is missing four books of the Torah?*

[Comments the Talmud:] *The cases are not comparable. In the case of a Torah scroll missing a sheet of parchment, the Torah is incomplete (Rashi: It is called a* Sefer Torah *and is lacking). In the case of the single* Chumash, *it is perfect and lacking nothing.*

The Law Follows Moshe

TEXT 7

Tszafnat Pane'ach, Ibid.

אם בדבר אשר הגדול והקטן שוים – אם גם בזה יש מעלה להגדול
על הקטן . . ויש בזה אריכות גדול בכמה מקצועות בש"ס . . עיין
גיטין דף ס' [ע"א].

The disagreement between Korach and Moshe is over whether the greater has an advantage over the lesser even in their shared common denominator ... The Talmud speaks at great length on this matter in various areas ... see Gittin 60a.

Man and Animal

Political Philosophy

TEXT 8

Bamidbar (Numbers) 18:1-2

וַיֹּאמֶר ה' אֶל אַהֲרֹן אַתָּה וּבָנֶיךָ וּבֵית אָבִיךָ אִתָּךְ תִּשְׂאוּ אֶת עֲוֹן
הַמִּקְדָּשׁ וְאַתָּה וּבָנֶיךָ אִתָּךְ תִּשְׂאוּ אֶת עֲוֹן כְּהֻנַּתְכֶם: וְגַם אֶת אַחֶיךָ
מַטֵּה לֵוִי שֵׁבֶט אָבִיךָ הַקְרֵב אִתָּךְ וְיִלָּווּ עָלֶיךָ וִישָׁרְתוּךָ וְאַתָּה וּבָנֶיךָ
אִתָּךְ לִפְנֵי אֹהֶל הָעֵדֻת:

G-d said to Aaron: You, your sons, and your father's house shall bear the iniquity associated with the Sanctuary, and you and your sons with you shall bear the iniquity associated with your kehunah, *with the priesthood. Also your brethren, the tribe of Levi, your father's tribe, draw close to you, and they shall join you and minister to you, and you and your sons with you, before the Tent of Testimony.*

TEXT 9

Talmud Tractate Tamid, 26b

דתנן שבצפון שער הניצוץ כמין אכסדרא היה ועלייה בנוי על גבה,
שהכהנים שומרים מלמעלה והלוים מלמטה. . . מנא הני מילי?
דתנו רבנן 'וילוו עליך וישרתוך'. . הא כיצד כהנים שומרים מלמעלה
ולוים מלמטה.

In the north of the Temple was the Shaar HaNitzutz,
the "Chamber of the Spark," built like a sort of porch,
and there was an upper chamber built on top of it,
where the priests would keep watch from above and
the Levites from below ... This is how "they shall join
you and minister to you": While the Kohanim *watch*
from above, the Levites guard from below.

The Leader Is Everything

TEXT 10

The Lubavitcher Rebbe, Likutei Sichot, vol. 4, p. 1051-1052

און דאס איז געווען טענת קרח: "כי כל העדה כולם קדושים"—אין
די זאכן וואס אלע אידן זיינען גלייך קדושים, אין קיום המצוות
"מדוע תתנשאו"—פארוואס איז בנוגע די ענינים וואוסאלע זיינען
גלייך, די ענינים פשוטים—דארפן אויך איד מקבל זיין זיי דורך
משה רבינו?

Rabbi Menachem Mendel Schneerson
1902–1994

The towering Jewish leader of the 20th century, known as "the Lubavitcher Rebbe," or simply as "the Rebbe." Born in southern Ukraine, the Rebbe escaped Nazi-occupied Europe, arriving in the U.S. in June 1941. The Rebbe inspired and guided the revival of traditional Judaism after the European devastation, impacting virtually every Jewish community the world over. The Rebbe often emphasized that the performance of just one additional good deed could usher in the era of Mashiach. The Rebbe's scholarly talks and writings have been printed in more than 200 volumes.

This was the claim of Korach: "The entire congregation is holy." That is, regarding matters in which all Jews are equally holy, in the performance of the physical commandments that every Jew does equally (Moshe wraps tefillin, *at the physical level, exactly the same as Korach or any other Jew), "why do you raise yourself above them?" Why, asks Korach, does every Jew need to receive direction from Moshe, even in the common denominators?*

TEXT 11

Likutei Sichot, Ibid., p. 1051 and footnote 16

און אזוי איז עס אויך געווען ביי משה רבינו, אז דורך זיין התנשאות
האבן אידן באקומען דורך אים ניט בלויז השגות נעלות וכדומה,
נאר אויך אלע זייערע ענינים, ביז צו ענינים פשוטים ביותר (און
דאס זעלבע איז אויך ביי אתפשטותא דמשה שבכל דרא ודרא, ביי
די נשיאים, ראשי בני ישראל) אז אלע אנשי דורם דארפן מקבל זיין
זייער חיות דורך די נשיאים כי כל ישראל הם קומה אחת שלימה
וראשי הדור כוללים את הנשמות של כל אנשי הדור כמו שהראש
כולל חיות כל אברי הגוף, ולכן ההשפעה שממשיכים לאנשי דורם
הוא בכל מציאות אנשי הדור, וגם בענינים הפשוטים, כמו שאברי
הגוף מקבלים כל חיותם, גם החיות שבצפרנים, מהמוח שבראש.

The fact that even the simple needs of every Jew are provided by the leader of the generation was also true of Moses. Inasmuch as he was "raised up above the congregation," the Jewish people acquired through him not just lofty insight and the like, but all of their needs, even the simplest ones. And this is the case with the Moses of every generation—the very life of the generation comes through the "heads of the Children of Israel."

This is because the Jewish people are compared to one complete human form, and the heads of the generation are the soul-root for all Jews of their time, just as the head is the nerve center of the entire body. Thus, the nourishment he grants to the members of his generation are in every area of life, even in the simplest things, just as the life-force of even the fingernails stems from the brain.

Man and Beast

TEXT 12

Tsafnat Pane'ach to the Torah, Numbers 16:3

אם בשר החמור והבהמה שוים לאדם, רצונו לומר אם החי של האדם הוא מציאות אחת להחי של בהמה ורק בשכל הוא משונה, או גם בכל הדברים הוא גדול.

The argument between Korach and Moses hinges on whether the flesh of a donkey or another animal is similar to that of a human. That is, whether the animal life of a human is identical to that of a beast except for his intellect, or whether he is different even in bodily matters.

Plato's Primordial World

TEXT 13

Tsafnat Pane'ach to the Torah, Bamidbar 16:3

וזה באמת הוא גדר אפיקורוס של שיטת אפלטון הידוע, דגדר החי
—אדם ובהמה שווים, לגדר הצומח—אדם ובהמה וצומח שוים,
ובגדר הדומם — הכל שווים, דכל בני אדם לבד משכלם הם שווים
וכן בעלי חיים, וזה כפירה בכל התורה, אז נקרא קרח אפיקורוס
כמבואר בירושלמי סנהדרין פ"י [ה"א].

In truth, Korach's position is the same heresy as the well-known heresy of Plato. Plato says that when it comes to animal life, both humans and beasts are equal. When it comes to plant life—that is, the phenomenon of growth—man, animal, and plant are equal. And in experience of inanimate matter, everything is equal. Thus, the "higher" creations are merely successive additions to the lower ones; inanimate matter that grows is a plant, a plant that can also move is an animal, and an animal that can think is a man.

In other words, Plato maintains that men deprived of their intellects are equal with one another and indistinguishable from animals. This runs contrary to the entire Torah, which is why Korach is called a heretic in the Jerusalem Talmud.

TEXT 14A

Maimonides, Guide for the Perplexed 2:13

Rabbi Moshe ben Maimon
(Maimonides, Rambam)
1135–1204

Halachist, philosopher, author, and physician. Maimonides was born in Córdoba, Spain. After the conquest of Córdoba by the Almohads, he fled Spain and eventually settled in Cairo, Egypt. There, he became the leader of the Jewish community and served as court physician to the vizier of Egypt. He is most noted for authoring the *Mishneh Torah*, an encyclopedic arrangement of Jewish law, and for his philosophical work, *Guide for the Perplexed*. His rulings on Jewish law are integral to the formation of halachic consensus.

דעות האנשים בקדמות העולם או חידושו לכל מי שיאמין שיש שם אלוק נמצא—הם שלש דעות . . .

והדעת השני הוא דעת כל מי ששמענו ענינו וראינו דבריו מן הפילוסופים וזה שהם אומרים כי מן השקר שימציא האלוק דבר לא מדבר ואי אפשר גם כן אצלם שיפסיד דבר אל לא דבר—רצוני לומר שאי אפשר שיתהוה נמצא אחד בעל חומר וצורה מהעדר החומר ההוא העדר גמור ולא יפסד אל העדר החומר ההוא העדר גמור - ותאר האלוק אצלם בשהוא יכול על זה כתארו בשהוא יכול לקבץ בין שני ההפכים בעתה אחת או יברא כמותו ית׳ או יתגשם או יברא מרובע קטרו שוה לצלעו ומה שדומה לזה מן הנמנעות. והמובן מדבריהם - שהם אומרים כמו שאין לאות בחוקו להיותו בלתי ממציא הנמנעות - כי לנמנע טבע קים אינו מפעולת פועל ולזה אי אפשר לשנותו - כן אין לאות בחוקו בשלא יוכל להמציא דבר מלא דבר שזה מכת הנמנעות כולם.

ולזה יאמינו שיש חומר אחד נמצא קדמון כקדמות האלוה לא ימצא הוא זולת החומר ולא החומר ימצא זולתו. ולא יאמינו שהחומר במעלתו יתברך במציאות אבל הוא סיבת מציאותו והוא לא על דרך משל כחומר ליוצר או הברזל לנפח והוא אשר יברא בו מה שירצה פעם יציר ממנו שמים וארץ ופעם יציר ממנו זולת זה. ואנשי זאת הכת יחלקו אל כתות אין תועלת לזכרון כתותיהם ודעותיהם בזה המאמר; אבל שורש זאת הכת הכולל—מה שזכרתי לך. ואפלטון גם כן זו היא האמנתו . . . וזהו הדעת השני.

Among those who believe in the existence of G-d, there are three different theories with regard to the question of whether the Universe is eternal or not. . . .

The Second Theory—the theory of all philosophers, whose opinions and works are known to us, is this: It is impossible to assume that G-d produced anything from nothing, or that He reduces anything to nothing; that is to say, it is impossible that an object consisting of matter and form should be produced when that matter is absolutely absent, or that it should be destroyed in such a manner that that matter be absolutely no longer in existence.

To say of G-d that He can produce a thing from nothing or reduce a thing to nothing is, according to the opinion of these philosophers, the same as if we were to say that He could cause one substance to simultaneously possess two opposite properties, or produce another being like Himself, or change Himself into a body, or produce a square the diagonal of which will be equal to its side, or similar impossibilities.

The philosophers thus believe that it is no defect in the Supreme Being, that He does not produce impossibilities, for the nature of that which is impossible is constant—it does not depend on the action of an agent, and for this reason it cannot be changed. Similarly there is, according to them, no defect in the greatness of G-d, when He is unable to produce a thing from nothing, because they consider this as one of the impossibilities.

They therefore assume that a certain substance has coexisted with G-d from eternity in such a manner that neither G-d existed without that substance nor the latter without G-d. But they do not maintain that the existence of that substance equals in rank that of G-d: for G-d is the cause of that existence, and the substance is in the same relation to G-d as the clay is to the potter, or the iron to the smith: G-d can do with it what He pleases; at one time He forms of it heaven and earth, at another time He forms some other thing.

The followers of this theory are divided into different schools, whose opinions and principles it is useless to discuss here: but what I have mentioned is common to all of them. Plato maintains the same opinion ... This is the second theory.

TEXT 14B

Ibid.

הדעת הראשון - הוא דעת כל מי שהאמין תורת 'משה רבינו עליו
השלום—הוא שהעולם בכללו—רצוני לומר כי כל נמצא מלבד
האלוה יתברך—האלוק המציאו אחר ההעדר הגמור המוחלט
ושהאלוה יתברך לבדו היה נמצא ולא דבר בלעדיו לא מלאך ולא
גלגל ולא מה שבתוך הגלגל; ואחר כן המציא כל אלה הנמצאות
כפי מה שהם ברצונו וחפצו לא מדבר...

וזו היא אחת הדעות והיא—יסוד תורת משה רבינו עליו השלום
בלי ספק והיא שניה ליסוד היחוד—לא יעלה בדעתך זולת זה.
ואברהם אבינו עליו השלום התחיל לגלות זה הדעת אשר הביאו
אליו העיון; ולזה היה קורא "בשם ה' א-ל עולם". וכבר הראה זה
הדעת באמרו "קונה שמים וארץ".

The First Theory, those who follow the Law of Moses, our Teacher, maintain that the entire Universe, i.e., everything except G-d, has been brought by Him into existence out of non-existence. In the beginning, G-d alone existed, and nothing else; neither angels, nor spheres, nor the things that are contained within the spheres existed. From that state of nothingness, G-d then created all existing things such as they are, by His will and desire. . . .

This is the first theory, and it is undoubtedly a fundamental principle of the Law of our teacher Moses; it is of primary importance second only to the principle of G-d's unity. Do not follow any other theory. Abraham, our father, was the first who taught it, after he had established it by philosophical research. He proclaimed, therefore, "the name of the Lord the G-d of the Universe"; and he had previously expressed this theory in the words, "Owner of heaven and earth."

A Confused Time

TEXT 15

The Lubavitcher Rebbe, Hayom Yom, Entry for 8 Iyar

אֵלֶּה שְׁמוֹת הָאֲנָשִׁים אֲשֶׁר שָׁלַח מֹשֶׁה לָתוּר אֶת הָאָרֶץ וַיִּקְרָא מֹשֶׁה לְהוֹשֵׁעַ בִּן נוּן יְהוֹשֻׁעַ:

והנה חסידים זיינען שלוחים פון רבי'ן... איז אז מ'טוט, איז מען מקושר, איז דאמאלט איז ער אין אלץ מקושר: עם גערט א חסיד, עסט א חסיד, שלאפט א חסיד.

Chasidim are agents of the Rebbe ... If the Chasid actively discharges his mission, he is bound up with his Rebbe, bound up in his entire being, "There walks a Chasid, there eats a Chasid, there sleeps a Chasid."

11

CHUKAT

Moses's Double Standard

The Drawbacks of Authenticity

PARSHAH OVERVIEW
Chukat

Moses is taught the laws of the red heifer, whose ashes purify a person who has been contaminated by contact with a dead body.

After forty years of journeying through the desert, the people of Israel arrive in the wilderness of Zin. Miriam dies, and the people thirst for water. G-d tells Moses to speak to a rock and command it to give water. Moses gets angry at the rebellious Israelites and strikes the stone. Water issues forth, but Moses is told by G-d that neither he nor Aaron will enter the Promised Land.

Aaron dies at Hor Hahar and is succeeded in the high priesthood by his son Elazar. Venomous snakes attack the Israelite camp after yet another eruption of discontent in which the people "speak against G-d and Moses"; G-d tells Moses to place a brass serpent upon a high pole, and all who will gaze heavenward will be healed. The people sing a song in honor of the miraculous well that provided them water in the desert.

Moses leads the people in battles against the Emorite kings Sichon and Og (who seek to prevent Israel's passage through their territory) and conquers their lands, which lie east of the Jordan.

Between a Rock and a Hard Place

Romancing the Stone

TEXT 1

Bamidbar (Numbers) 20:7-12

וַיְדַבֵּר ה' אֶל מֹשֶׁה לֵּאמֹר:

קַח אֶת הַמַּטֶּה וְהַקְהֵל אֶת הָעֵדָה אַתָּה וְאַהֲרֹן אָחִיךָ וְדִבַּרְתֶּם אֶל הַסֶּלַע לְעֵינֵיהֶם וְנָתַן מֵימָיו וְהוֹצֵאתָ לָהֶם מַיִם מִן הַסֶּלַע וְהִשְׁקִיתָ אֶת הָעֵדָה וְאֶת בְּעִירָם:

וַיִּקַּח מֹשֶׁה אֶת הַמַּטֶּה מִלִּפְנֵי ה' כַּאֲשֶׁר צִוָּהוּ:

וַיַּקְהִלוּ מֹשֶׁה וְאַהֲרֹן אֶת הַקָּהָל אֶל פְּנֵי הַסָּלַע וַיֹּאמֶר לָהֶם שִׁמְעוּ נָא הַמֹּרִים הֲמִן הַסֶּלַע הַזֶּה נוֹצִיא לָכֶם מָיִם:

וַיָּרֶם מֹשֶׁה אֶת יָדוֹ וַיַּךְ אֶת הַסֶּלַע בְּמַטֵּהוּ פַּעֲמָיִם וַיֵּצְאוּ מַיִם רַבִּים וַתֵּשְׁתְּ הָעֵדָה וּבְעִירָם:

וַיֹּאמֶר ה' אֶל מֹשֶׁה וְאֶל אַהֲרֹן יַעַן לֹא הֶאֱמַנְתֶּם בִּי לְהַקְדִּישֵׁנִי לְעֵינֵי בְּנֵי יִשְׂרָאֵל לָכֵן לֹא תָבִיאוּ אֶת הַקָּהָל הַזֶּה אֶל הָאָרֶץ אֲשֶׁר נָתַתִּי לָהֶם:

G-d spoke to Moses, saying:

"Take the staff and assemble the congregation, you and your brother Aaron, and speak to the rock in their presence so that it will give forth its water. You shall bring forth water for them from the rock and give the congregation and their livestock to drink."

Moses took the staff from before the Lord as He had commanded him.

Moses and Aaron assembled the congregation in front of the rock, and he said to them, "Now listen, you rebels; can we draw water for you from this rock?"

Moses raised his hand and struck the rock with his staff twice, when an abundance of water gushed forth, and the congregation and their livestock drank.

G-d said to Moses and Aaron, "Because you did not have faith in Me to sanctify Me in the eyes of the Children of Israel, therefore you shall not bring this assembly into the Land that I have given them."

TEXT 2

Bamidbar (Numbers) 11:22-23

הֲצֹאן וּבָקָר יִשָּׁחֵט לָהֶם וּמָצָא לָהֶם אִם אֶת כָּל דְּגֵי הַיָּם יֵאָסֵף לָהֶם וּמָצָא לָהֶם:
וַיֹּאמֶר ה' אֶל מֹשֶׁה הֲיַד יְקֹוָק תִּקְצָר עַתָּה תִרְאֶה הֲיִקְרְךָ דְבָרִי אִם לֹא:

"If sheep and cattle were slaughtered for them, would it suffice for them? If all the fish of the sea were gathered for them, would it suffice for them?"

Then G-d said to Moses, "Is My power limited? Now you will see if My word comes true for you or not!"

Faltering and Infallible

TEXT 3A

Mishlei (Proverbs) 24:16

כִּי שֶׁבַע יִפּוֹל צַדִּיק וָקָם וּרְשָׁעִים יִכָּשְׁלוּ בְרָעָה:

Seven times the righteous man falls and gets up, while the wicked are tripped by one misfortune.

TEXT 3B

Rabbi David Altschuler, Metsudat David, ad loc.

Rabbi David Altschuler
1687–1769
Biblical commentator. Rabbi Altschuler, a renowned Polish rabbi, wrote two biblical commentaries that are considered crucial to Bible study: the *Metsudat David* expounds upon the meaning of the text, and *Metsudat Tsion* provides definitions. After he died a martyr's death, his works were published by his son, Rabbi Hillel Altschuler, under the name *Metsudot*.

"כִּי שבע". כי אף אם הצדיק נופל שבע פעמים יחזור ויקום אבל הרשעים הם הנכשלים מבלי תקומה בבוא עליהם הרעה.

"Seven." For even though the righteous may fall seven times, he will return and rise. However, the wicked are those who stumble without rising once evil befalls them.

TEXT 4

Rabbi Shneur Zalman of Liadi,
Introduction to Shaar Hayichud Veha'emunah, Part II of Tanya

Rabbi Shneur Zalman of Liadi
(Alter Rebbe)
1745–1812
Chasidic rebbe, halachic authority, and founder of the Chabad movement. The Alter Rebbe was born in Liozna, Belarus, and was among the principal students of the Magid of Mezeritch. His numerous works include the *Tanya*, an early classic containing the fundamentals of Chabad Chasidism, and *Shulchan Aruch HaRav*, an expanded and reworked code of Jewish law.

אך הנה ידוע ליודעים טעמא דקרא, מאי דכתיב: כי שבע יפול צדיק וקם ובפרט שהאדם נקרא מהלך, ולא עומד וצריך לילך ממדרגה למדרגה, ולא לעמוד במדרגה אחת לעולם.

ובין מדרגה למדרגה, טרם שיגיע למדרגה עליונה ממנה, הוא בבחינת נפילה ממדרגתו הראשונה אך: כי יפול לא יוטל, כתיב ואינה נקראת נפילה אלא לגבי מדריגתו הראשונה, ולא לגבי שאר כל אדם, חס ושלום.

Now, those who are familiar with the esoteric meaning of Scripture know [the explanation of] the verse "For a tzaddik falls seven times and rises up again. "Especially since man is called "mobile" and not "static," he must ascend from level to level and not remain forever at one plateau.

Between one level and the next, before he can reach the higher one, he is in a state of decline from the previous level. Yet, it is written, "Though he falls, he shall not be utterly cast down." It is considered a decline only in comparison with his former state, and not, G-d forbid, in comparison with all other men.

The Individual and the Community

Solipsism and the Selfie in Scripture

TEXT 5

Mishnah Tractate Sanhedrin, 4:5

Mishnah
The first authoritative work of Jewish law that was codified in writing. The Mishnah contains the oral traditions that were passed down from teacher to student; it supplements, clarifies, and systematizes the commandments of the Torah. Due to the continual persecution of the Jewish people, it became increasingly difficult to guarantee that these traditions would not be forgotten. Rabbi Yehudah Hanasi therefore redacted the Mishnah at the end of the second century. It serves as the foundation for the Talmud.

לְפִיכָךְ נִבְרָא אָדָם יְחִידִי, לְלַמֶּדְךָ, שֶׁכָּל הַמְאַבֵּד נֶפֶשׁ אַחַת מִיִּשְׂרָאֵל, מַעֲלֶה עָלָיו הַכָּתוּב כְּאִלּוּ אִבֵּד עוֹלָם מָלֵא.וְכָל הַמְקַיֵּם נֶפֶשׁ אַחַת מִיִּשְׂרָאֵל, מַעֲלֶה עָלָיו הַכָּתוּב כְּאִלּוּ קִיֵּם עוֹלָם מָלֵא.

וּמִפְּנֵי שְׁלוֹם הַבְּרִיּוֹת, שֶׁלֹּא יֹאמַר אָדָם לַחֲבֵרוֹ אַבָּא גָּדוֹל מֵאָבִיךָ. וְשֶׁלֹּא יְהוּ מִינִין אוֹמְרִים, הַרְבֵּה רָשֻׁיּוֹת בַּשָּׁמָיִם. וּלְהַגִּיד גְּדֻלָּתוֹ שֶׁל הַקָּדוֹשׁ בָּרוּךְ הוּא, שֶׁאָדָם טוֹבֵעַ כַּמָּה מַטְבְּעוֹת בְּחוֹתָם אֶחָד וְכֻלָּן דּוֹמִין זֶה לָזֶה, וּמֶלֶךְ מַלְכֵי הַמְּלָכִים הַקָּדוֹשׁ בָּרוּךְ הוּא טָבַע כָּל אָדָם בְּחוֹתָמוֹ שֶׁל אָדָם הָרִאשׁוֹן וְאֵין אֶחָד מֵהֶן דּוֹמֶה לַחֲבֵרוֹ. לְפִיכָךְ כָּל אֶחָד וְאֶחָד חַיָּב לוֹמַר, בִּשְׁבִילִי נִבְרָא הָעוֹלָם.

It was for this reason that man was first created as one person [Adam], to teach you that anyone who destroys a life is considered by Scripture to have destroyed an entire world; and anyone who saves a life is as if he saved an entire world."

And also, to promote peace among the creations; that no man would say to his friend, "My ancestors are greater than yours."

And also, so that heretics will not say, "there are many rulers up in heaven."

And also, to express the grandeur of the Holy One [blessed be He]: For a man strikes many coins from the same die, and all the coins are alike. But the King, the King of Kings, the Holy One [blessed be He] strikes every man from the die of the first man, and yet no man is quite like his friend.

Therefore, every person must say, "For my sake the world was created."

Bespoke Prophecy

TEXT 6

Zohar, vol. 1, 102b-103a

רַבִּי יְהוּדָה פָּתַח "נוֹדָע בַּשְּׁעָרִים בַּעְלָהּ בְּשִׁבְתּוֹ עִם זִקְנֵי אָרֶץ". תָּא חֲזֵי, קוּדְשָׁא בְּרִיךְ הוּא אִסְתַּלַּק בִּיקָרֵיהּ דְּאִיהוּ גָּנִיז וְסָתִים בְּעִילּוּיָא סַגְיָא. לָאו אִיתֵי בְּעָלְמָא וְלָא הֲוָה מִן יוֹמָא דְּאִתְבְּרֵי עָלְמָא דְּיָכִיל לְקַיְּימָא עַל חָכְמָתָא דִּילֵיהּ וְלָא יָכִיל לְקַיְּימָא בֵּיהּ. בְּגִין דְּאִיהוּ גָּנִיז וְסָתִים וְאִסְתַּלַּק לְעֵילָּא לְעֵילָּא, וְכֻלְּהוּ עִלָּאֵי וְתַתָּאֵי לָא יָכְלִין לְאִתְדַבְּקָא... וְאַתְּ אָמַרְתְּ נוֹדָע בַּשְּׁעָרִים בַּעְלָהּ?

אֶלָּא וַדַּאי נוֹדָע בַּשְּׁעָרִים בַּעְלָהּ דָּא קוּדְשָׁא בְּרִיךְ הוּא דְּאִיהוּ אִתְיְדַע וְאִתְדָּבַּק לְפוּם מַה דִּמְשַׁעֵר בְּלִבֵּיהּ כָּל חַד כְּמָה דְּיָכִיל לְאִתְדַּבְּקָא בְּרוּחָא דְחָכְמְתָא. וּלְפוּם מַה דִּמְשַׁעֵר בְּלִבֵּיהּ הָכִי אִתְיְדַע בְּלִבֵּיהּ. וּבְגִינֵי כָךְ נוֹדָע בַּשְּׁעָרִים בְּאִנּוּן שְׁעָרִים.

Zohar

The seminal work of kabbalah, Jewish mysticism. The *Zohar* is a mystical commentary on the Torah, written in Aramaic and Hebrew. According to the Arizal, the *Zohar* contains the teachings of Rabbi Shimon bar Yocha'i who lived in the Land of Israel during the second century. The *Zohar* has become one of the indispensable texts of traditional Judaism, alongside and nearly equal in stature to the Mishnah and Talmud.

Rabbi Yehudah said: The verse states, "Her Husband is known in the gates, when he sits among the elders of the land." Come and behold, the Holy One, blessed be He, was exalted in His glory, because He is hidden, concealed, and greatly elevated. Since the creation of the world, nobody has ever been able to grasp His wisdom, and to comprehend it, for He is hidden, concealed, exalted to the highest of highs. Above and below, nothing is able to cleave to Him . . . Yet, you say that "her Husband is known in the gates"?

Rather, "Her Husband is known in the gates (she'arim)" indeed refers to the Holy One, blessed be He, Who makes Himself known and attaches Himself to everyone according to the extent that one measures (mesha'er) in one's heart, each person, as much as he is able to attach himself to the spirit of wisdom. According to the extent one measures in [his] heart, does He make himself known in [his] heart. Therefore, He is known in the gates (she'arim)—in those measures (she'aarim).

The Social Self

TEXT 7

Talmud Tractate Sanhedrin, 17b

Babylonian Talmud

A literary work of monumental proportions that draws upon the legal, spiritual, intellectual, ethical, and historical traditions of Judaism. The 37 tractates of the Babylonian Talmud contain the teachings of the Jewish sages from the period after the destruction of the Second Temple through the fifth century CE. It has served as the primary vehicle for the transmission of the Oral Law and the education of Jews over the centuries; it is the entry point for all subsequent legal, ethical, and theological Jewish scholarship.

תניא כל עיר שאין בה עשרה דברים הללו אין תלמיד חכם רשאי
לדור בתוכה בית דין מכין ועונשין וקופה של צדקה נגבית בשנים
ומתחלקת בשלשה ובית הכנסת ובית המרחץ וביהכ"ס רופא ואומן
ולבלר (וטבח) ומלמד תינוקות.
משום רבי עקיבא אמרו אף מיני פירא מפני שמיני פירא מאירין
את העינים.

It has been taught: A scholar should not reside in a city where the following ten things are not found: A court of justice that imposes flagellation and decrees penalties; a charity fund collected by two and distributed by three; a synagogue; public baths; a convenience; a circumciser; a surgeon, a notary; a slaughterer; and a schoolmaster.

Rabbi Akiva is quoted [as including] also several kinds of fruit [in the list], because these are beneficial to the eyesight.

TEXT 8A

Mishnah Tractate Avot, 2:4

הלל אומר אל תפרוש מן הצבור.

Hillel would say: Do not separate yourself from the community.

TEXT 8B

Rabbi Yisrael Lifshitz, Tiferet Yisrael, Avot, ad loc.

(א) שלא יפרוש ממנהגי הצבור, וכמו שאמר חז"ל אזל לקרתא אזל לנמוסוא. (ב) כשמתכנסין לקבוע שיעור לימוד, או להתפלל, או להתיעץ בעסק מצוה או בצרכי צבור, לא יאמר יחליטו הם מה שירצו ואני מתרצה בכך או בכך, רק צריך ליעץ לטובת הצבור ולסייע בכל דבר לעבודת ה'. (ג) כשהצבור ולא הוא שרויים בצער, ירגיש צרתם כאילו הוא עצמו גם כן שרוי עמם בצער. (ד) כשמתפלל על עצמו, ישתתף את עצמו בתפלתו עמהן, לכלול את עצמו בכלל כל הנצרכין בזאת.

1. He ought not to depart from the communal custom, as our sages have said, "When one goes to a city, one should adopt its mannerisms."

2. When [the community] gathers to set up a public study session, or to pray, or to discuss religious matters or communal affairs, he should not say,

"Let them decide as they will; I am content with either way." Rather, he should offer counsel for the benefit of the community, and to support whatever promotes the service of G-d.

3. When the community suffers, but he is [unaffected], he should nevertheless feel their predicament as though he were experiencing the same pain.

4. When praying for himself, he should include himself with them in his prayers, to include himself among all people who share the same need.

TEXT 9

The Lubavitcher Rebbe, Likutei Sichot, vol. 33, p. 110

כי הגדר דציבור הוא לא שותפות של כמה וכמה יחידים, אלא מציאות חדשה.

A community is defined not as a partnership between a large number of individuals, but a new entity.

Rabbi Menachem Mendel Schneerson
1902–1994

The towering Jewish leader of the 20th century, known as "the Lubavitcher Rebbe," or simply as "the Rebbe." Born in southern Ukraine, the Rebbe escaped Nazi-occupied Europe, arriving in the U.S. in June 1941. The Rebbe inspired and guided the revival of traditional Judaism after the European devastation, impacting virtually every Jewish community the world over. The Rebbe often emphasized that the performance of just one additional good deed could usher in the era of Mashiach. The Rebbe's scholarly talks and writings have been printed in more than 200 volumes.

Sanctifying G-d's Name

TEXT 10

Vayikra (Leviticus) 22:32

וְלֹא תְחַלְּלוּ אֶת שֵׁם קָדְשִׁי וְנִקְדַּשְׁתִּי בְּתוֹךְ בְּנֵי יִשְׂרָאֵל אֲנִי
ה' מְקַדִּשְׁכֶם:

You shall not desecrate My Holy Name. I shall be sanctified amidst the Children of Israel. I am G-d Who sanctifies you.

TEXT 11A

Maimonides, Mishneh Torah, Laws of Yesodei HaTorah 5:1-2

Rabbi Moshe ben Maimon (Maimonides, Rambam) 1135–1204
Halachist, philosopher, author, and physician. Maimonides was born in Córdoba, Spain. After the conquest of Córdoba by the Almohads, he fled Spain and eventually settled in Cairo, Egypt. There, he became the leader of the Jewish community and served as court physician to the vizier of Egypt. He is most noted for authoring the *Mishneh Torah*, an encyclopedic arrangement of Jewish law, and for his philosophical work, *Guide for the Perplexed*. His rulings on Jewish law are integral to the formation of halachic consensus.

כל בית ישראל מצווין על קדוש השם הגדול הזה שנאמר ונקדשתי
בתוך בני ישראל. ומוזהרין שלא לחללו שנאמר ולא תחללו את
שם קדשי. כיצד כשיעמוד עובד כוכבים ויאנוס את ישראל לעבור
על אחת מכל מצות האמורות בתורה או יהרגנו יעבור ואל יהרג
שנאמר במצות אשר יעשה אותם האדם וחי בהם. וחי בהם ולא
שימות בהם. ואם מת ולא עבר הרי זה מתחייב בנפשו.
במה דברים אמורים בשאר מצות חוץ מעבודת כוכבים וגלוי עריות
ושפיכת דמים. אבל שלש עבירות אלו אם יאמר לו עבור על אחת
מהן או תהרג. יהרג ואל יעבור.

All of Israel are commanded regarding the sanctification of [G-d's] great name, as the verse states, "And I shall be sanctified amidst the Children of Israel." Also, they are warned against desecrating [His holy name], as [the above verse] states, "And they shall not desecrate My holy name."

What is implied? Should a Gentile arise and force a Jew to violate one of the Torah's commandments at the pain of death, he should violate the commandment rather than be killed, because it is stated concerning the mitzvot, "which a man will perform and live by them." [They were given so that] one may live by them and not die because of them. If a person dies rather than transgresses, he is held accountable for his life.

When does the above apply? With regard to other mitzvot, with the exception of the worship of other gods, forbidden sexual relations, and murder. If one is ordered, "Transgress one of them or be killed," one should sacrifice his life rather than transgress any of these three sins.

TEXT 11B

Maimonides, Ibid., 5:11

יש דברים אחרים שהן בכלל חילול השם. והוא שיעשה אותם
אדם גדול בתורה ומפורסם בחסידות דברים שהבריות מרננים
אחריו בשבילם.

ואף על פי שאינן עבירות הרי זה חילל את השם כגון שלקח ואינו
נותן דמי המקח לאלתר. והוא שיש לו ונמצאו המוכרים תובעין
והוא מקיפן. או שירבה בשחוק או באכילה ושתיה אצל עמי הארץ
וביניהן. או שדבורו עם הבריות אינו בנחת ואינו מקבלן בסבר פנים
יפות אלא בעל קטטה וכעס. וכיוצא בדברים האלו הכל לפי גדלו
של חכם צריך שידקדק על עצמו ויעשה לפנים משורת הדין.

וכן אם דקדק החכם על עצמו והיה דבורו בנחת עם הבריות ודעתו
מעורבת עמהם ומקבלם בסבר פנים יפות ונעלב מהם ואינו עולבם.
מכבד להן ואפילו למקילין לו. ונושא ונותן באמונה. ולא ירבה
באריחות עמי הארץ וישיבתן. ולא יראה תמיד אלא עוסק בתורה
עטוף בציצית מוכתר בתפילין ועושה בכל מעשיו לפנים משורת
הדין. והוא שלא יתרחק הרבה ולא ישתומם. עד שימצאו הכל
מקלסין אותו ואוהבים אותו ומתאוים למעשיו הרי זה קידש את ה׳
ועליו הכתוב אומר ״ויאמר לי עבדי אתה ישראל אשר בך אתפאר״.

*There are other deeds that are also included in [the cat-
egory of] the desecration of [G-d's] name if performed
by a person of great Torah stature who is renowned
for his piety—i.e., deeds that, although they are not
transgressions, [will cause] people to speak disparag-
ingly of him. This also constitutes the desecration of
[G-d's] name.*

For example, a person who purchases [merchandise] and does not pay for it immediately, although he possesses the money, and thus the sellers demand payment and he pushes them off; a person who jests immoderately; or who eats and drinks near or among the common people; or whose conduct with other people is not gentle and he does not receive them with a favorable countenance, but rather contests with them and vents his anger; and the like. Everything depends on the stature of the sage. [The extent to which] he must be careful with himself and go beyond the measure of the law [depends on the level of his Torah stature].

[The converse is] also [true]. When a sage is stringent with himself, speaks pleasantly with others, his social conduct is [attractive] to others, he receives them pleasantly, he is humbled by them and does not humble them in return, he honors them—even though they disrespect him—he does business faithfully, and does not frequently accept the hospitality of the common people or sit with them, and at all times is seen only studying Torah, wrapped in tzitzit, *crowned with* tefillin, *and carrying out all his deeds beyond the measure of the law—provided he does not separate too far [from normal living] and thus become forlorn—to the extent that all praise him, love him, and find his deeds attractive—such a person sanctifies [G-d's] name. The verse "And He said to me, 'Israel, you are My servant, in whom I will be glorified'" refers to him.*

Keeping the Double Standard

Return to the Rock

TEXT 12

Rashi on Bamidbar 20:12

Rabbi Shlomo Yitzchaki
(Rashi)
1040–1105
Most noted biblical and
Talmudic commentator.
Born in Troyes, France,
Rashi studied in the famed
yeshivot of Mainz and
Worms. His commentaries
on the Pentateuch and
the Talmud, which focus
on the straightforward
meaning of the text, appear
in virtually every edition
of the Talmud and Bible.

"יען לא האמנתם בי". גלה הכתוב שאלולי חטא זה בלבד היו
נכנסין לארץ, כדי שלא יאמרו עליהם כעון שאר דור המדבר, שנגזר
עליהם שלא יכנסו לארץ, כך היה עון משה ואהרן. והלא "הצאן
ובקר ישחט" קשה מזו, אלא לפי שבסתר חסך עליו הכתוב, וכאן
שבמעמד כל ישראל, לא חסך עליו הכתוב מפני קדוש השם.

"Because you did not have faith in Me." Scripture reveals that if it were not for this sin alone, they would have entered the land, so that it should not be said of them, "The sin of Moses and Aaron was like the sin of the generation of the desert against whom it was decreed that they should not enter [the land]."

But was not [the question asked by Moses,] "If sheep and cattle were slaughtered for them ..." a more grievous [sin] than this?

However, there Moses said it in private, so Scripture spares him [and refrains from punishing him]. Here, on the other hand, it was said in the presence of all

Israel, so Scripture does not spare him because of the sanctification of the Name.

TEXT 13A

The Lubavitcher Rebbe, Likutei Sichot, vol. 28, p. 128

נאר דער טעם דערויף ווערט אנגעדייט אין פסוק "יען לא האמנתם
בי להקדישני לעיני בני ישראל", און ווי רש"י איז דאס מבאר, איז
דערפאר איז דער חטא מער חמור ווי די טענה פון משה רבינו
"הצאן ובקר ישחט להם"—וויל דארט "לפי שבסתר חסך עליו
הכתוב, וכאן שבמעמד כל ישראל לא חסך עליו הכתוב מפני
קידוש השם".
דאס הייסט אז ווען רעדט זיך ווען וועגן אן ענין פון קידוש השם
אדער הפכו, איז נוגע בלויז ווי אזוי דאס ווערט אויסגעטייטשט
דורך אנדערע.

The reason [for Moses's punishment] is alluded to in the verse, "Because you did not have faith in Me to sanctify Me in the eyes of the Children of Israel." As Rashi explains it, it is for this reason that this sin was more serious than Moshe's protest to G-d that "if sheep and cattle were slaughtered for them, would it suffice for them?" There, "Because it was in private, the Torah spared him [judgment], but here, [acting] in the presence of all Israel, the Torah did not spare him, because of the opportunity for the sanctification of G-d's name."

That is to say, in cases where a Kiddush Hashem, or the opposite, is at stake, all that is relevant is how one's actions are interpreted by others.

TEXT 13B

Likutei Sichot, Ibid., p. 125-128

The [Previous] Rebbe related: It was before noontime on a Thursday, the first of the month of Tamuz [1927], that he received word he would be released from imprisonment and sent into exile for three years in the town of Kostroma. As such, he was informed, once freed later that day, he would be allowed to spend six hours with his family but would have to leave the city at night and proceed to Kostroma.

Because it was already Thursday, the Rebbe asked, when would he arrive at Kostroma?

He was to arrive on Shabbat, was the answer.

The Rebbe replied that he would not travel on Shabbat under any circumstances. It was only after intense lobbying of the upper circles of government had its effect that the Rebbe was permitted to travel on Sunday, the third of Tamuz (until which time he remained in prison) . . .

On the face of it, it seems most odd: Why did the Rebbe take such an adamant stance against the original travel plans and instead place himself at such risk? One would think that the very first thing he should have done was to immediately leave the (danger of the) prison, after which he could look for a way to a avoid traveling on Shabbat.

Perhaps the explanation is this: The dilemma was not whether he should or should not give up his life for [the observance of] Shabbat; the question was about Kiddush Hashem *or* Chillul Hashem.

The goal of those who arrested the Rebbe was to disrupt his work in strengthening Judaism. Had the Rebbe not immediately opposed the order to travel as soon as he was freed, as they desired (so that the Rebbe would set out before Shabbat)—[the Soviets] would have attained a victory: The Rebbe had "agreed" to travel on Shabbat.

Anyone hearing of this agreement would not have known all of the previously discussed considerations (about the secretive efforts to ensure that the Rebbe would not need to travel on Shabbat) . . .

A Light Unto the Nations

TEXT 14A

The Lubavitcher Rebbe, Likutei Sichot, vol. 27, p. 258

A Jewish person's existence serves as witness to G-d, as it is written, "You are my witnesses." That is, through one's good, upright conduct, one testifies to G-d's goodness and uprightness, so to speak.

TEXT 14B

Talmud Tractate Yoma, 86a

ואהבת את ה' אלהיך שיהא שם שמים מתאהב על ידך שיהא
קורא ושונה ומשמש ת"ח ויהא משאו ומתנו בנחת עם הבריות מה
הבריות אומרות עליו אשרי אביו שלמדו תורה אשרי רבו שלמדו
תורה אוי להם לבריות שלא למדו תורה פלוני שלמדו תורה ראו
כמה נאים דרכיו כמה מתוקנים מעשיו עליו הכתוב אומר ויאמר לי
עבדי אתה ישראל אשר בך אתפאר.

"And thou shall love the Lord your G-d": The Name of Heaven should be beloved because of you.

If someone studies Scripture and Mishnah, and attends on the disciples of the wise, is honest in business, and speaks pleasantly to persons, what do people then say of him?

"Happy the father who taught him Torah, happy the teacher who taught him Torah; woe unto people who have not studied the Torah; for this man has studied the Torah; look how fine his ways are, how righteous his deeds!"

Of him does Scripture say, "And He said unto me, 'You are My servant, Israel, in whom I will be glorified?'"

What's in a Good Name?

TEXT 15A

Mishnah Tractate Avot, 4:13

> רבי שמעון אומר: שלושה כתרים הם: כתר תורה וכתר כהונה וכתר מלכות. וכתר שם טוב עולה על גביהן.

Rabbi Shimon would say: There are three crowns—the crown of Torah, the crown of priesthood, and the crown of sovereignty—but the crown of a good name surmounts them all.

TEXT 15B

The Lubavitcher Rebbe, Torat Menachem, vol. 24 (5719 vol. 1), p. 122

אימתי היא מעלת "כתר שם טוב" – בהיותו "על גביהן", היינו,
בבואו לאחרי ג' הכתרים שלפני זה.

שם טוב כשלעצמו אינו מעלה גדולה כל כך (וכאמור שזהו ענין
חיצוני), ולכן לא נמנה בתור כתר רביעי, כיון שלעצמו אינו מעלה
גדולה. אבל בשעה שישנם ג' הכתרים תורה כהונה ומלכות,
ולאחריהם – "על גביהן" – בא כתר שם טוב, אזי הוא "עולה",
שהוא נעלה יותר מג' הכתרים עצמם.

*When is the "crown of a good name" superior? When
it "surmounts the others," that is when it comes [on top
of and] after the three preceding crowns.*

*In and of itself, a good reputation is not that great a
quality (as previously discussed, it is a superficial quality) and therefore it is not listed as a fourth crown. . . .
However, once there are the three "crowns" of Torah,
Priesthood, and Sovereignty, and following them—
"surmounting them"—the crown of a good name, then
it "surmounts" them [in the sense that] it is higher than
the three crowns on their own.*

A Zealous Act

Extreme Measures for Extreme Times

PARSHAH OVERVIEW
Balak

Balak, the king of Moab, summons the prophet Balaam to curse the people of Israel. On the way, Balaam is berated by his donkey, who sees, before Balaam does, the angel that G-d sends to block their way. Three times, from three different vantage points, Balaam attempts to pronounce his curses; each time, blessings issue forth instead. Balaam also prophesies on the end of the days and the coming of Mashiach.

The people fall prey to the charms of the daughters of Moab and are enticed to worship the idol Peor. When a high-ranking Israelite official publicly takes a Midianite princess into a tent, Pinchas kills them both, stopping the plague raging among the people.

Death by Zealot

The Story

TEXT 1A

Bamidbar (Numbers) 25:1-6

וַיֵּשֶׁב יִשְׂרָאֵל בַּשִּׁטִּים וַיָּחֶל הָעָם לִזְנוֹת אֶל בְּנוֹת מוֹאָב:

וַתִּקְרֶאןָ לָעָם לְזִבְחֵי אֱלֹהֵיהֶן וַיֹּאכַל הָעָם וַיִּשְׁתַּחֲווּ לֵאלֹהֵיהֶן:

וַיִּצָּמֶד יִשְׂרָאֵל לְבַעַל פְּעוֹר וַיִּחַר אַף ה' בְּיִשְׂרָאֵל:

וַיֹּאמֶר ה' אֶל מֹשֶׁה קַח אֶת כָּל רָאשֵׁי הָעָם וְהוֹקַע אוֹתָם ה' נֶגֶד הַשָּׁמֶשׁ וְיָשֹׁב חֲרוֹן אַף ה' מִיִּשְׂרָאֵל:

וַיֹּאמֶר מֹשֶׁה אֶל שֹׁפְטֵי יִשְׂרָאֵל הִרְגוּ אִישׁ אֲנָשָׁיו הַנִּצְמָדִים לְבַעַל פְּעוֹר:

וְהִנֵּה אִישׁ מִבְּנֵי יִשְׂרָאֵל בָּא וַיַּקְרֵב אֶל אֶחָיו אֶת הַמִּדְיָנִית לְעֵינֵי מֹשֶׁה וּלְעֵינֵי כָּל עֲדַת בְּנֵי יִשְׂרָאֵל וְהֵמָּה בֹכִים פֶּתַח אֹהֶל מוֹעֵד:

Israel settled in Shittim, and the people began to commit harlotry with the daughters of the Moabites.

They invited the people to the sacrifices of their gods, and the people ate and prostrated themselves to their gods.

Israel became attached to Baal Peor, and the anger of G-d flared against Israel.

G-d said to Moses, "Take all the leaders of the people and hang them before the god, facing the sun, and then the flaring anger of G-d will be removed from Israel.

Moses said to the judges of Israel, "Each of you shall kill the men who became attached to Baal Peor.

Then an Israelite man came and brought the Midianite woman to his brethren, before the eyes of Moses and before the eyes of the entire congregation of the Children of Israel, while they were weeping at the entrance of the Tent of Meeting.

TEXT 1B

Ibid., v. 7-9

וַיַּרְא פִּינְחָס בֶּן אֶלְעָזָר בֶּן אַהֲרֹן הַכֹּהֵן וַיָּקָם מִתּוֹךְ הָעֵדָה וַיִּקַּח
רֹמַח בְּיָדוֹ:
וַיָּבֹא אַחַר אִישׁ יִשְׂרָאֵל אֶל הַקֻּבָּה וַיִּדְקֹר אֶת שְׁנֵיהֶם אֵת אִישׁ יִשְׂרָאֵל
וְאֶת הָאִשָּׁה אֶל קֳבָתָהּ וַתֵּעָצַר הַמַּגֵּפָה מֵעַל בְּנֵי יִשְׂרָאֵל:
וַיִּהְיוּ הַמֵּתִים בַּמַּגֵּפָה אַרְבָּעָה וְעֶשְׂרִים אָלֶף:

Pinchas the son of Elazar the son of Aaron the Kohen saw this, arose from the congregation, and took a spear in his hand.

He went after the Israelite man into the chamber and drove [it through] both of them; the Israelite man, and the woman through her stomach, and the plague ceased from the Children of Israel.

Those that died in the plague numbered twenty-four thousand.

TEXT 1C

Ibid., v. 10-13

וַיְדַבֵּר ה' אֶל מֹשֶׁה לֵּאמֹר:

פִּינְחָס בֶּן אֶלְעָזָר בֶּן אַהֲרֹן הַכֹּהֵן הֵשִׁיב אֶת חֲמָתִי מֵעַל בְּנֵי יִשְׂרָאֵל בְּקַנְאוֹ אֶת קִנְאָתִי בְּתוֹכָם וְלֹא כִלִּיתִי אֶת בְּנֵי יִשְׂרָאֵל בְּקִנְאָתִי:

לָכֵן אֱמֹר הִנְנִי נֹתֵן לוֹ אֶת בְּרִיתִי שָׁלוֹם:

וְהָיְתָה לּוֹ וּלְזַרְעוֹ אַחֲרָיו בְּרִית כְּהֻנַּת עוֹלָם תַּחַת אֲשֶׁר קִנֵּא לֵאלֹקָיו וַיְכַפֵּר עַל בְּנֵי יִשְׂרָאֵל:

G-d spoke to Moses, saying,

"Pinchas the son of Elazar the son of Aaron the Kohen has turned My anger away from the Children of Israel by his zealously avenging Me among them, so that I did not destroy the Children of Israel because of My zeal.

"Therefore, say, 'I hereby give him My covenant of peace.

"It shall be for him and for his descendants after him [as] an eternal covenant of priesthood, because he was zealous for his G-d and atoned for the Children of Israel.'"

The Detailed Version

TEXT 2A

Talmud Tractate Sanhedrin, 82a-b

הלך שבטו של שמעון אצל זמרי בן סלוא אמרו לו הן דנין דיני
נפשות ואתה יושב ושותק מה עשה עמד וקיבץ כ"ד אלף מישראל
והלך אצל כזבי אמר לה השמיעי לי אמרה לו בת מלך אני וכן צוה לי
אבי לא תשמעי אלא לגדול שבהם אמר לה אף הוא נשיא שבט הוא
ולא עוד אלא שהוא גדול ממנו שהוא שני לבטן והוא שלישי לבטן
תפשה בבלוריתה והביאה אצל משה אמר לו בן עמרם זו אסורה
או מותרת ואם תאמר אסורה בת יתרו מי התירה לך נתעלמה ממנו
הלכה... וכתיב וירא פנחס בן אלעזר מה ראה אמר רב ראה מעשה
ונזכר הלכה אמר...לא כך לימדתני...הבועל את כותית קנאין פוגעין
בו אמר לו קריינא דאיגרתא איהו ליהוי פרוונקא...וכיון שהגיע
אצל שבטו של שמעון אמר היכן מצינו שבבטו של לוי גדול משל
שמעון אמרו הניחו לו אף הוא לעשות צריכי נכנס התירו פרושין
את הדבר.

Babylonian Talmud
A literary work of monumental proportions that draws upon the legal, spiritual, intellectual, ethical, and historical traditions of Judaism. The 37 tractates of the Babylonian Talmud contain the teachings of the Jewish sages from the period after the destruction of the Second Temple through the fifth century CE. It has served as the primary vehicle for the transmission of the Oral Law and the education of Jews over the centuries; it is the entry point for all subsequent legal, ethical, and theological Jewish scholarship.

The tribe of Simeon went to Zimri, son of Salu, their leader, and said to him: They are judging cases of capital law and executing us and you are sitting and are silent? What did Zimri do? He arose and gathered twenty-four thousand people from the Children of Israel, and went to Cozbi, daughter of Zur, princess of Midian, and said to her, "Submit to me and engage in intercourse with me."

She said to him, "I am the daughter of a king, and this is what my father commanded me: Submit only to the greatest of them."

Zimri said to her, "I, too, am the head of a tribe; moreover, I am greater than Moses, as he is the second of the womb and he is the third of the womb."

He seized her by her forelock, brought her before Moses, and said, "Son of Amram, is this woman forbidden or permitted? And if you say that she is forbidden, then who permitted to you the daughter of Yitro?

The halachah eluded Moses... And it is written thereafter, "And Pinchas, son of Elazar, son of Aaron the priest, saw and arose from the midst of the congregation and took a spear in his hand."

What did Pinchas see? Rav says: He saw the incident taking place before him and he remembered the halachah. He said to Moses, "Did you not teach me that one who engages in intercourse with a Gentile woman, zealots strike him?" Moses said to him, "Let the one who reads the letter be the agent to fulfill its contents"... Once he reached the tribe of Simeon he said: Where did we find that the tribe of Levi is greater than that of Simeon? They said, "Allow him to enter; like us, he, too, is entering to attend to his needs—the pious have permitted this."

Six Miracles

TEXT 2B

Ibid.

אמר רבי יוחנן ששה נסים נעשו לו לפנחס אחד שהיה לו לזמרי
לפרוש ולא פירש ואחד שהיה לו לדבר ולא דבר ואחד שכוון
בזכרותו של איש ובנקבותה של אשה ואחד שלא נשמטו מן
הרומח ואחד שבא מלאך והגביה את המשקוף ואחד שבא מלאך
והשחית בעם.

Rabbi Yochanan says: Six miracles were performed for Pinchas when he killed Zimri. One is that Zimri should have separated himself from Cozbi, and he did not separate himself. And one is that Zimri should have spoken out and he did not speak. And one is that Pinchas directed the spear precisely to the male genitals of Zimri and to the female genitals of Cozbi. And one is that Zimri and Cozbi did not fall from the spear. And one is that an angel came and raised the lintel of that chamber so that Pinchas could emerge holding them aloft on the spear. And one is that an angel came and caused destruction among the people, distracting them from interfering with the actions of Pinchas.

Strict Circumstances

TEXT 3

Talmud Tractate Sanhedrin, 81b-82a

מתני': ....והבועל ארמית קנאין פוגעין בו **גמ:**...אמר רבי חסדא הבא
לימלך אין מורין לו איתמר נמי אמר רבה בר בר חנה אמר רבי יוחנן
הבא לימלך אין מורין לו ולא עוד אלא שאם פירש זמרי והרגו פנחס
נהרג עליו נהפך זמרי והרגו לפנחס אין נהרג עליו שהרי רודף הוא.

The Mishnah teaches that one who engages in intercourse with an Aramean woman is among those liable to be killed by zealots . . . Rav Chisda says: Concerning one who comes to consult with the court when he sees a Jewish man engaging in intercourse with a Gentile woman, the court does not instruct him that it is permitted to kill the transgressor.

It was also stated that Rabba bar bar Chana says in the name of Rabbi Yochanan: Concerning one who comes to consult with the court, the court does not instruct him that it is permitted to kill the Jewish man engaging in intercourse with a Gentile woman. Moreover, if Zimri had separated himself from the woman and only then had Pinchas killed him, Pinchas would have been executed for killing him, because it is permitted for zealots to kill only while the transgressor is engaged in the act of intercourse. Furthermore, if Zimri would have turned and killed Pinchas in self-defense, he would not have been executed for killing him, as Pinchas was a pursuer.

TEXT 4

Maimondies, Mishneh Torah, Hilchot Isurei Biah 12:4-5

כָּל הַבּוֹעֵל כּוּתִית בֵּין דֶּרֶךְ חַתְנוּת בֵּין דֶּרֶךְ זְנוּת אִם בְּעָלָהּ בְּפַרְהֶסְיָא וְהוּא שֶׁיִּבְעֹל לְעֵינֵי עֲשָׂרָה מִיִּשְׂרָאֵל אוֹ יֶתֶר אִם פָּגְעוּ בּוֹ קַנָּאִין וַהֲרָגוּהוּ הֲרֵי אֵלּוּ מְשֻׁבָּחִין וּזְרִיזִין [ו.] וְדָבָר זֶה הֲלָכָה לְמֹשֶׁה מִסִּינַי הוּא. רְאָיָה לְדָבָר זֶה מַעֲשֵׂה פִּינְחָס בְּזִמְרִי:

וְאֵין הַקַּנַּאי רַשַּׁאי לִפְגֹּעַ בָּהֶן אֶלָּא בִּשְׁעַת מַעֲשֶׂה כְּזִמְרִי שֶׁנֶּאֱמַר "וְאֶת הָאִשָּׁה אֶל קֳבָתָהּ". אֲבָל אִם פֵּרַשׁ אֵין הוֹרְגִין אוֹתוֹ. וְאִם הֲרָגוֹ נֶהֱרַג עָלָיו. וְאִם בָּא הַקַּנַּאי לִטֹּל רְשׁוּת מִבֵּית דִּין לְהָרְגוֹ אֵין מוֹרִין לוֹ וְאַף עַל פִּי שֶׁהוּא בִּשְׁעַת מַעֲשֶׂה. וְלֹא עוֹד אֶלָּא אִם בָּא הַקַּנַּאי לַהֲרֹג אֶת הַבּוֹעֵל וְנִשְׁמַט הַבּוֹעֵל וְהָרַג הַקַּנַּאי כְּדֵי לְהַצִּיל עַצְמוֹ מִיָּדוֹ אֵין הַבּוֹעֵל נֶהֱרַג עָלָיו.

Rabbi Moshe ben Maimon
(Maimonides, Rambam)
1135–1204

Halachist, philosopher, author, and physician. Maimonides was born in Córdoba, Spain. After the conquest of Córdoba by the Almohads, he fled Spain and eventually settled in Cairo, Egypt. There, he became the leader of the Jewish community and served as court physician to the vizier of Egypt. He is most noted for authoring the *Mishneh Torah*, an encyclopedic arrangement of Jewish law, and for his philosophical work, *Guide for the Perplexed*. His rulings on Jewish law are integral to the formation of halachic consensus.

Whenever a Jewish man has relations with a Gentile woman in public, i.e., the relations are carried out in the presence of ten or more Jews, if a zealous person strikes him and kills him, he [the zealot] is considered praiseworthy and ardent. [This applies whether the relations were] in the context of marriage or licentious in nature. This matter is a halachah conveyed to Moses at Sinai. Support for this can be derived from Pinchas's slaying of Zimri.

The zealous person can strike [the fornicators] only at the time of relations, as was the case with regard to Zimri, as the verse states, "[He pierced] the woman into her stomach." If, however, [the transgressor] withdraws, he should not be slain. Indeed, if the zealous person slays him, he may be executed [as a murderer].

TEXT 5

Rabbi Moshe Isserlis, glosses to the Shulchan Aruch, Choshen Mishpat, §46

Rabbi Moshe Isserlis
(Rama)
1525–1572
Halachist. Rama served as rabbi in Krakow, Poland, and is considered the definitive authority on Jewish law among Ashkenazic Jewry. Rama authored glosses (known as the *Mapah*) on the Shulchan Aruch and *Darchei Moshe*, a commentary on the halachic compendium *Arbaah Turim*.

הבא על העכו"ם בפרהסיא לעיני י' ישראלים קנאין פוגעין בו ומותרין להרגו ודוקא בשעת מעשה אבל אם פירש אסור להרגו ודוקא שהתרו בו ולא פירש ודוקא שבא הקנאי להורגו מעצמו אבל אם שאל לבית דין אין מורים לו כך.

One who engages in relations with a Gentile in public, in the presence of at least ten Jewish people, is liable to be killed by zealots. This applies only during the act of intercourse. But after the fact, it is forbidden to kill him. This applies only if he was warned and nevertheless did not desist. This applies only if the zealot only came to kill on his own accord. If, however, he asked the bet din *whether or not he may kill, they do not permit him to kill.*

Crossing the Line

What's in a Sin?

TEXT 6A

Rabbi Shneur Zalman of Liadi, Tanya Iggeret Hateshuvah ch. 6

Rabbi Shneur Zalman of Liadi (Alter Rebbe) 1745–1812

Chasidic rebbe, halachic authority, and founder of the Chabad movement. The Alter Rebbe was born in Liozna, Belarus, and was among the principal students of the Magid of Mezeritch. His numerous works include the *Tanya*, an early classic containing the fundamentals of Chabad Chasidism, and *Shulchan Aruch HaRav*, an expanded and reworked code of Jewish law.

והנה יעקב חבל נחלתו כתיב. על דרך משל כמו החבל שראשו א'
למעלה וראשו השני למטה אם ימשוך אדם בראשו השני ינענע
וימשך אחריו גם ראשו הראשון כמה שאפשר לו להמשך. וככה
ממש בשרש נשמת האדם ומקורה..הוא ממשיך ומוריד השפעתה
על ידי מעשיו הרעים ומחשבותיו עד תוך היכלות הסטרא אחרא
כביכול שמשם מקבל מחשבותיו ומעשיו. ומפני שהוא הוא
הממשיך להם ההשפעה לכן הוא נוטל חלק בראש וד"ל...וזוהי
בחינת גלות השכינה כביכול להשפיע להיכלות הסטרא אחרא
אשר שנאה נפשו יתברך. וכשהאדם עושה תשובה נכונה אזי מסלק
מהם ההשפעה שהמשיך במעשיו ומחשבותיו. כי בתשובתו מחזיר
השפעת השכינה למקומה.

It is written, "Jacob is the rope of [G-d's] heritage." The analogy [compares the soul of a Jew] to a rope, with one end above and the other end below. When one pulls the lower end, he will drag after it the higher end as well, as far as it can be pulled.

It is exactly so with regard to the root of the soul of man and its source… Through one's evil deeds and thoughts, one draws down the life-force into the chambers of the sitra achra, *as it were, from which he* receives his thoughts and deeds. Because it is he, the sinful individual, who draws the flow of vitality into [the chambers of the sitra achra], it is he who receives the greatest portion from them. This will suffice for the understanding…This is an expression of the "Exile of the Divine Presence," as it were…viz., [G-d's] granting [supplementary measures of] life-force to the chambers of the sitra achra that He despises.

But when the sinner repents appropriately, he then removes from them the life-force that he had drawn into them through his deeds and thoughts, for by his repentance he returns the flow issuing from the Shechinah to its proper place.

TEXT 6B

Ibid., ch. 6

והאיך נשברה רוח הסטרא אחרא, כשהלב נשבר ונדכה וכו' והאיך נשבר הלב ונדכה . . . הוא להיות ממארי דחושבנא בעומק הדעת להעמיק דעתו ובינתו שעה אחת בכל יום או לילה לפני תיקון חצות להתבונן במה שפעל ועשה בחטאיו, בחינת גלות השכינה כנ"ל וגרם לעקור נשמתו ונפשו האלקית מחיי החיים ברוך הוא והורידה למקום הטומאה והמות, הן היכלות הסטרא אחרא ונעשית בבחינת מרכבה אליהם לקבל מהם שפע וחיות להשפיע לגופו, כנ"ל.

How is the spirit of the sitra achra *broken? When the heart is "broken and contrite," etc. And how is the heart to be broken and humbled? . . . [It] is achieved through being a "master of accounting" with all the profundity of one's mind. One should concentrate his intellect and understanding deeply for a period every day, or at night before* Tikkun Chatzot, *to contemplate how through his sins he has brought about the exile of the Divine Presence, as noted above, and caused his spirit and divine soul to be uprooted from the Divine Source of all Life, and demeaned it to a place of defilement and death, namely, the chambers of the* sitra achra, *[his soul] becoming a vehicle for them, receiving from them vitality to endow his body.*

TEXT 7

Rabbi Shalom Dovber Schneersohn, Sefer Hamaamarim 5657, p.269-7

Spiritually speaking, the father's seed stems from the core and essence of his intellectual ability, as it is in the depths of his soul. Therefore, in its transmission, his offspring is endowed with an intellectual soul that mirrors that of the father, to the point that the son may even surpass the ability of the father. This is because in his seed is transmitted the entire unrevealed core of the father's soul. As a perfect being, the soul has no measure or limit to what can be expressed from it. All

Rabbi Shalom Dovber Schneersohn
(Rashab)
1860–1920

Chasidic rebbe. Rabbi Shalom Dovber became the fifth leader of the Chabad movement upon the passing of his father, Rabbi Shmuel of Lubavitch. He established the Lubavitch network of *yeshivot* called Tomchei Temimim. He authored many volumes of Chasidic discourses and is renowned for his lucid and thorough explanations of kabbalistic concepts.

limits apply only to already revealed expressions of the soul.

TEXT 8

The Lubavitcher Rebbe, Likutei Sichot, vol 8, p. 15

Rabbi Menachem Mendel Schneerson
1902–1994

The towering Jewish leader of the 20th century, known as "the Lubavitcher Rebbe," or simply as "the Rebbe." Born in southern Ukraine, the Rebbe escaped Nazi-occupied Europe, arriving in the U.S. in June 1941. The Rebbe inspired and guided the revival of traditional Judaism after the European devastation, impacting virtually every Jewish community the world over. The Rebbe often emphasized that the performance of just one additional good deed could usher in the era of Mashiach. The Rebbe's scholarly talks and writings have been printed in more than 200 volumes.

דער חטא פון ביאות אסורות איו הארבער פון אנדערע עבירות, דערמיט וואס "ביאה" פארנעמט דעם גאנצן מענטשן און נעמט זיך פון נפש ווי זי איז העכער פון כחות הגלויים [וואס דערפאר קען מען מוליד זיין א בן וואס האט אלע כחות הנפש, ביז עס קען זיין "יפה כח הבן מכח האב" ווארום די הולדה נעמט זיך פון עצם הנפש ווי זי איז העכער פון כחות הגלויים — און בעצם נפשו איז דאך דער אב שלם בכל כחותיו], קומט דאך אויס, אז דורך א ביאה אסורה ר"ל טראגט מען אריין אן ענין עצמי אין קליפה (ניט וי ביי אנדערע עבירות, וואו דער חוטא איו מכניס אין קליפה בלויז יענע כחות פון נפש האלקית וועלכע זיינען שייך צו דער פעולה פרטית).

The sin of forbidden relations is worse than other sins because it consumes the entire person and draws from the depths of the soul. [This is why it is possible for one to father a son who is greater than himself, for the child's birth stems from the core of the father's soul, and at its core, the soul is, in fact, perfect in every way]. It emerges, then, that by engaging in forbidden relations, one drags the core of his soul into the forces of evil (unlike other sins, where one drags into evil only the specific faculty which pertains to that specific sin).

Night and Day

TEXT 9

Siddur Tehillat Hashem, Havdalah Prayer

ברוך אתה ה אלקינו מלך העולם המבדיל בין קודש לחול בין אור
לחשך בין ישראל לעמים בין יום השביעי לששת ימי המעשה ברוך
אתה ה' המבדיל בין קודש לחול.

*Blessed are You, Lord our G-d, King of the universe,
who makes a distinction between sacred and mundane,
between light and darkness, between Israel and the nations, between the seventh day and the six workdays.
Blessed are You, G-d, who makes a distinction between
sacred and mundane.*

Siddur

The siddur is the Jewish prayer book. It was originally developed by the sages of the Great Assembly in the 4th century BCE, and later reconstructed by Rabban Gamliel after the destruction of the Second Temple. Various authorities continued to add prayers, from then until contemporary times. It includes praise of God, requests for personal and national needs, selections of the Bible, and much else. Various Jewish communities have slightly different versions of the siddur.

TEXT 10

Maimonides, Mishneh Torah, Hilchot Isurei Biah 12:7

עָוֹן זֶה אַף עַל פִּי שֶׁאֵין בּוֹ מִיתַת בֵּית דִּין אַל יְהִי קַל בְּעֵינֶיךָ, אֶלָּא יֵשׁ
בּוֹ הֶפְסֵד שֶׁאֵין בְּכָל הָעֲרָיוֹת כְּמוֹתוֹ. שֶׁהַבֵּן מִן הָעֶרְוָה בְּנוֹ הוּא לְכָל
דָּבָר וּבִכְלַל יִשְׂרָאֵל נֶחְשָׁב אַף עַל פִּי שֶׁהוּא מַמְזֵר וְהַבֵּן מִן הַכּוּתִית
אֵינוֹ בְּנוֹ שֶׁנֶּאֱמַר "כִּי יָסִיר אֶת בִּנְךָ מֵאַחֲרַי" מֵסִיר אוֹתוֹ מִלִּהְיוֹת
אַחֲרֵי ה':

Although this transgression is not punishable by execution by the court, it should not be regarded lightly, for it leads to a detriment that has no parallel among all the other forbidden sexual relations. For a child conceived from any other forbidden sexual union is [the father's] son with regard to all matters and is considered a member of the Jewish people, even if he is a mamzer. A son conceived by a Gentile woman, by contrast, is not considered his son, as is derived from the verse, "For he shall sway your son away from following Me." She turns him away from being one of those who follow G-d.

Transcending Torah

Off the Radar

TEXT 11

Talmud Yerushalmi Tractate Makot, 2:6

שאלו לחכמה חוטא מהו עונשו אמרו להם חטאים תרדף רעה
שאלו לנבואה חוטא מהו עונשו אמרה להן הנפש החוטאת היא
תמות שאלו לתורה חוטא מהו עונשו אמרה להן יביא קרבן ויתכפר
להן שאלו לקודשא בריך הוא חוטא מהו עונשו אמר להן יעשו
תשובה ויתכפר לו. היינו דכתיב על כן יורה חטאים בדרך יורה
לחטאים דרך עשות תשובה.

Jerusalem Talmud

A commentary to the Mishnah, compiled during the fourth and fifth centuries. The Jerusalem Talmud predates its Babylonian counterpart by 100 years and is written in both Hebrew and Aramaic. While the Babylonian Talmud is the most authoritative source for Jewish law, the Jerusalem Talmud remains an invaluable source for the spiritual, intellectual, ethical, historical, and legal traditions of Judaism.

They asked wisdom, "What is the punishment for a sinner?" It answered, "Sinners should be chased by evil."

They asked prophecy, "What is the punishment for a sinner?" It answered, "A sinner should die."

They asked the Torah, "What is the punishment for a sinner?" It answered, "[The sinner] should bring a sacrifice and it will be forgiven." They asked G-d, "What is the punishment for a sinner?" He responded, "Let him do teshuvah and he will be forgiven."

This is the meaning of the verse, "Therefore, He leads sinners on the road." He leads sinners on the path of teshuvah.

Deep Zealotry

TEXT 12

Tana Devei Eliyahu, ch. 1

Tana Devei Eliyahu
A Midrashic work, sometimes referred to as *Seder Eliyahu*. Midrash is the designation of a particular genre of rabbinic literature usually forming a running commentary on specific books of the Bible. This work deals with the divine precepts, their rationales, and the importance of knowledge of Torah, prayer, and repentance. The work is divided into two sections *(Sedarim): Eliyahu Rabah* and *Eliyahu Zuta*.

אמר לי רבי שני דברים יש לי בלבבי, ואני אוהבן אהבה גדולה, תורה וישראל. אבל איני יודע איזה מהן קודם. אמרתי לו, דרכן של בני אדם שאומרים תורה קדומה לכל. שנאמר ה' קנני ראשית דרכו (משלי) אבל הייתי אומר. ישראל קדושים קודמין. שנאמר קודש ישראל לה' ראשית תבואתו.

Rebbi said to me: "There are two things in my heart that I love with a great love. They are the Torah and the Jewish people. But I don't know which takes precedence over the other."

I said to him, "The Jewish people are accustomed to say, "The Torah precedes everything," as the verse states, "G-d acquired me at the beginning of His way." But I would say the Holy people of Israel take precedence. As the verse states, "Israel is holy to G-d, the first of His grain."

Only During the Act

TEXT 13

Rabbi Shalom Dovber Schneersohn of Lubavitch,
Sefer Hamaamarim 5670, p. 102-103

וכמו שאמר רז"ל אך על פי שחטא ישראל הוא דהנשמה האלקית
במה שיורדת רחמנא לצלן גם בעמקי הקליפות בריבוי חטאים
ועוונות רחמנא לצלן מעל מקום אינה נהפכת לרע חס ושלום, והרי
הוא רק בגלות ושביה, ועל ידי זה מתחלשת ונחשך אורה מאד
עד שיכול להיות שנכבה אורה וכמו בחייבי כריתות רחמנא לצלן
שנכרת משרשה כו', אבל אינה מתהפכת חס ושלום, שהרי אין לך
דבר שעומד בפני התשובה, שהתשובה מועלת על הכל . . . ונמצא
דגם בחינת ניצוץ הקדושה שנפל בדרך נפילה ושבירה אינו נעשה
רע גמור חס ושלום, וכל שכן שהנשמה האלקית אינה נהפכת לרע
חס ושלום, הרי שהטוב אינו נהפך לרע כו'.

Our sages have said, *"Though one has sinned, he re-mains a Jew." Though through much sin the G-dly soul descends to the ranks of evil, G-d forbid, nevertheless, it is not converted to evil, G-d forbid; it is merely in exile and imprisonment, which weakens its light until it can even be extinguished. This is the case with sins punishable by excision, G-d forbid, wherein the soul is cut from its source, etc. Still, the soul is not converted to evil, for "Nothing stands in the way of teshuvah," for teshuvah can atone for everything... It emerges that a G-dly spark that has fallen [into kelipah] is not converted to evil, G-d forbid, and certainly the G-dly* soul does not become evil [through sin], G-d forbid. As a rule, good does not become evil, etc.

Priesthood

TEXT 14

The Lubavitcher Rebbe, Likutei Sichot, vol. 8, p. 15

און דאס איז אויך דער ביאור אין דעם וואס שכר פנחס איז "ברית
כהונת עולם"—אף על פי אז כהונה איז אן ענין פון טבע—וייל
וויבאלד אז דער חטא פון זמרי (וואס האט ארויסגעבראכט קנאות
פנחס) איז באשטאנען אין אראפנעמען די הבדלה שבין ישראל
לעמים, וואס איז בדוגמת "ויבדל גו' בין האור ובין החשך" כנ"ל,
דעריבער איז "תחת אשר קנא לאלקיו", האט ער באקומען דעם
שכר—מדה כנגד מדה, "והיתה לו ולזרעו אחריו ברית כהונת עולם."

This is why Pinchas was rewarded with "an eternal covenant of priesthood"—though priesthood is a matter determined at birth by nature: Because Zimri's sin (which evoked Pinchas's zealotry) involved crossing the divide between the Jewish people and the other nations, which are essentially divided just as G-d "divided between light and dark," therefore, "because he was zealous for his G-d" he was rewarded—measure for measure, that "it shall be for him and for his descendants after him [as] an eternal covenant of priesthood."

THE ROHR
Jewish Learning Institute

822 Eastern Parkway, Brooklyn, New York 11213

CHAIRMAN
Rabbi Moshe Kotlarsky
Lubavitch World Headquarters,
New York

PRINCIPAL BENEFACTOR
Mr. George Rohr
New York, NY

EXECUTIVE DIRECTOR
Rabbi Efraim Mintz

ADMINISTRATOR
Rabbi Dubi Rabinowitz

EXECUTIVE COMMITTEE
Rabbi Chaim Block
S. Antonio, TX
Rabbi Hesh Epstein
Columbia, SC
Rabbi Ronnie Fine
Montreal, Quebec
Rabbi Yosef Gansburg
Toronto, Ontario
Rabbi Shmuel Kaplan
Potomac, MD
Rabbi Yisrael Rice
S. Rafael, CA
Rabbi Avrohom Sternberg
New London, CT

TORAH STUDIES

CHAIRMAN
Rabbi Yosef Gansburg
Toronto, Ontario

MANAGING EDITOR
Rabbi Ahrele Loschak
Brooklyn, NY

ADMINISTRATOR
Rabbi Levi Kaplan
Brooklyn, NY

FOUNDING DIRECTOR
Rabbi Meir Hecht
Chicago, IL

STEERING COMMITTEE
Rabbi Levi Fogelman
Natick, MA
Rabbi Yaakov Halperin
Allentown, PA
Rabbi Nechemiah Schusterman
Peabody, MA
Rabbi Ari Sollish
Atlanta, GA

CONTENT EDITORS
Rabbi Shneur Broh
Brooklyn, NY
Rabbi Zalman Ives
Brooklyn, NY
Rabbi Sholom Ber Notik
Brooklyn, NY
Shmuel Loebenstein
Brooklyn, NY
Rabbi Boruch Werdiger
Jerusalem, Israel

MARKETING AND PR
Rabbi Zalman M. Abraham
Sheva Rivkin

TEXTBOOK DESIGN
Shternie Morozow
Rabbi Zalman Korf

COPYEDITING
Mr. Michael Barnett
Bel Air, MD

POWERPOINT DESIGN
Mrs. Bunie Chazan
Manchester, England
Rabbi Cheski Edelman
Olympia, WA

PRODUCTION
Rabbi Mendel Sirota
Brooklyn, NY

An affiliate of
Merkos L'Inyonei Chinuch
The Educational Arm of the Worldwide
Chabad Lubavitch Movement

JEWISH LEARNING INSTITUTE

THE JEWISH LEARNING MULTIPLEX

Brought to you by the Rohr Jewish Learning Institute

In fulfillment of the mandate of the Lubavitcher Rebbe, of blessed memory,
whose leadership guides every step of our work,
the mission of the Rohr Jewish Learning Institute is to transform
Jewish life and the greater community through the study of Torah,
connecting each Jew to our shared heritage of Jewish learning.

While our flagship program remains the cornerstone of our organization,
JLI is proud to feature additional divisions catering to specific populations,
in order to meet a wide array of educational needs.

THE ROHR JEWISH LEARNING INSTITUTE,
a subsidiary of *Merkos L'Inyonei Chinuch*,
is the adult education arm of the Chabad-Lubavitch Movement.

TORAH STUDIES

Torah Studies provides a rich and nuanced encounter with the weekly Torah reading.

MYSHIUR
TALMUD LEARNING INITIATIVE

MyShiur courses are designed to assist students in developing the skills needed to study Talmud independently.

SINAI SCHOLARS SOCIETY
IN PARTNERSHIP WITH CHABAD ON CAMPUS

This rigorous fellowship program invites select college students to explore the fundamentals of Judaism.

JLI TEENS
YOUNG SMART JEWISH

IN PARTNERSHIP WITH CTEEN: CHABAD TEEN NETWORK

Jewish teens forge their identity as they engage in Torah study, social interaction, and serious fun.

ROSHCHODESH society

The Rosh Chodesh Society gathers Jewish women together once a month for intensive textual study.

TORAHCafé

TorahCafe.com provides an exclusive selection of top-rated Jewish educational videos.

National JEWISH RETREAT
BRILLIANT LEARNING. NATURALLY.

This yearly event rejuvenates mind, body, and spirit with a powerful synthesis of Jewish learning and community.

the LAND & the SPIRIT
ISRAEL EXPERIENCE

Mission participants delve into our nation's rich past while exploring the Holy Land's relevance and meaning today.

JLI ACADEMY
PEDAGOGY • CURRICULUM • MARKETING

Select affiliates are invited to partner with peers and noted professionals, as leaders of innovation and excellence.

מכון שמואל

THE SAMI ROHR RESEARCH INSTITUTE

Machon Shmuel is an institute providing Torah research in the service of educators worldwide.